Twayne's United States Authors Series

Sylvia E. Bowman, *Editor*

INDIANA UNIVERSITY

Will Rogers

Will Rogers

WILL ROGERS

By E. PAUL ALWORTH, 1917—

University of Tulsa

 236

Twayne Publishers, Inc.   ::   New York

Library of Congress Cataloging in Publication Data

Alworth, E. Paul, 1917-
  Will Rogers, by E. Paul Alworth. New York, Twayne [c1974]
  140 p. port. 21 cm.
  (Twayne's United States authors series, TUSAS 236)
  Bibliography: p. 131 - 135.
  1. Rogers, Will, 1879-1935. 2. American wit and
humor — History and criticism.
PN2287.R74A7   791'.092'4   73-16415
ISBN O-8057-0634-8

Preface

Crackerbox philosophers, those purveyors of common sense and aphoristic humor, have long held a position of respect and admiration in America; but none of them was more beloved or held in higher esteem by his countrymen than Will Rogers. When he was killed in an airplane accident on August 15, 1935, virtually the entire nation went into mourning. He was only a private citizen, a motion picture actor, humorist, and political commentator; yet, on the occasion of his death, the President of the United States openly expressed his personal sorrow and grief, Congress halted its deliberations to pay tribute to his memory, and millions of Americans mourned as if a dear friend or relative had passed away.

With the passage of time, many of Will's aphorisms have become American folklore; and Rogers himself has become an American legend. Although his books are seldom read and his motion pictures are outdated, he himself has become part of the folk tradition. He is regarded as the symbol of the Common Man, a representative of the very best in American life. As the legend has developed, Will has become a Folk Hero, not unlike Abe Lincoln. The wisdom of the cowboy-philosopher identifies him as a true product of the American frontier, a man of "common sense" who was never deceived by political chicanery or misled by unmerited, temporary triumphs of people or causes not basically sound. Probably Will was not so sagacious as the legend would have us believe; but it is equally true that he could not have said and written such clever comments so long and so frequently as he did without being fundamentally wise.

Will's success as a humorist was in a large part due to the variety of mediums through which he reached his audience — vaudeville, newspapers, periodicals, lecture platform, and motion pictures. However, in this study I do not intend to examine him as a "role player" in any of the guises in which he appeared before the public;

nor do I attempt to evaluate his political or economic philosophy as expressed in his humor. Instead, I propose to examine the *humor* of Will Rogers and to establish a relationship between him and the crackerbox philosophers of the nineteenth century. I hope to demonstrate that he followed the same patterns of humor, expressed the same practical wisdom, and assumed the same posture of ignorance that characterized his predecessors. His humor was in the same tradition as that of Jack Downing, Hosea Biglow, Artemus Ward, Josh Billings, Mr. Dooley, and Mark Twain whose delightful fooling so amused and so educated their audiences. To this end, I have divided this study into four parts: (1) a brief examination of the life and the formative influences on the character of Will Rogers as a humorist; (2) a presentation of the opinions and attitudes which he held as expressed in his writings on both the national and international scenes; (3) a critical analysis of his character and his techniques and patterns of humor; and (4) the relationship of Will Rogers to the crackerbox philosophers before him.

As a result of this study I have come to believe that Will not only had a strong affinity for his predecessors, but also that he was the last of the crackerbox philosophers to speak to a national audience. For almost two hundred years, the United States had not been without a "horse-sense" humorist who could speak to and for the average American, articulating with wit the unspoken thoughts of the common people. But with Will's death in 1935, this traditional form of humor lost its last champion except on a regional basis. Just why this common-sense expression has lost its popularity is difficult to say, but apparently, among other things, mass education and mass media have generated a sophisticated audience for whom this kind of humor is unacceptable. Will Rogers was the last, although not the least, purveyor of this distinctive native expression; and because of his merits he certainly deserves consideration in the history of American humor.

E. PAUL ALWORTH

University of Tulsa

Acknowledgments

My chief source of information on Will Rogers was the Will Rogers Memorial, which is located on a hill overlooking the humorist's hometown of Claremore, Oklahoma. Here, before her untimely death last summer, Mrs. Paula McSpadden Love, a niece of the humorist and the curator of the Memorial, and her husband, Mr. Robert Love, have indexed and classified the vast amount of material sent to them by the Rogers' family and by friends and interested people from all parts of the world. Paula and Bob Love were not only kind enough to help me locate information pertinent to this study, but also they were instrumental in arranging for me to meet and interview both Will Rogers, Jr., and James Rogers, the humorist's sons. I am grateful for their help, their kindness, and their encouragement as I developed this study.

I also wish to acknowledge my indebtedness to Walter Blair and Jennette Tandy whose seminal works on American humor were invaluable to this study; and to Donald Day, whose collections of Will Rogers' humor were most helpful. My debt to these scholars goes far beyond the cited material.

Finally, I wish to express my gratitude to Will Rogers, Jr., and the Will Rogers Company for giving me permission to quote from Will's books and from his daily and weekly columns.

Contents

Chronology

1879   Will Rogers born November 4 at the Rogers ranch home near Claremore, Oklahoma.

1887-   Attended Drumgoole School near Chelsea; Presbyterian
1898   Mission School in Tahlequah; Harrell Institute in Muskogee; Willie Halsell College in Vinita; Scarlett College Institute in Neosho, Missouri; and Kemper Military Institute in Booneville, Missouri. Formal education ended in winter of the year when Rogers ran away from school to work on the Ewing ranch in Higgins, Texas.

1902   Managed Rogers ranch for his father. In the spring, traveled to South America with Dick Paris, a cowboy friend. After five months, traveled to South Africa.

1903   Toured South Africa with Texas Jack's Wild West Show as a trick rider and roper. Later joined Wirth Brothers Circus and toured Australia and New Zealand.

1904   Appeared with Colonel Mulhall's Wild West Show at the World's Fair in St. Louis.

1905   Traveled with the Mulhall Wild West Show to New York City. Stayed in New York and received first vaudeville contract as a trick-roping performer.

1908   Married Betty Blake, Rogers, Arkansas.

1911-   Birth of first son, Will Rogers, Jr. Traveled with vaudeville
1915   circuit which included tours both in the United States and Europe. Only daughter, Mary Amelia Rogers, born in 1913 Engaged by Florenz Ziegfeld to play in the Midnight Frolics. Second son, James Blake, was born in 1915.

1916   Joined the Ziegfeld Follies as a regular performer. Starred in the Follies for the next eleven years.

1919   Published first books: *The Cowboy Philosopher on the Peace Conference* and *The Cowboy Philosopher on Prohibition.*

Moved to California to work in the movies at the Goldwyn studio.

1922 Returned to New York. Became popular speaker at conventions, banquets, and group meetings in the New York area. Began weekly article for McNaught syndicate which continued to his death in 1935.

1924 Moved to California to make movies for the Hal Roach studio. Published *The Illiterate Digest.*

1926 Traveled to Europe for the *Saturday Evening Post.* Published *Letters of Self-Made Diplomat to His President.* Began to write his daily telegram, "Will Rogers Says" which was syndicated by McNaught.

1927 Published *There's Not a Bathing Suit in Russia.* Visited Mexico with Charles Lindbergh as a guest of Ambassador Dwight Morrow.

1929 Made first talking picture "They Had to See Paris" which established him as film star. Published *Ether and Me.*

1930 Began first regular series of radio broadcasts.

1931- Toured Central America for benefit of earthquake victims.
1932 Gave numerous benefits in the United States for drought sufferers in Southwest. Made trip to the Orient during the invasion of Manchuria by the Japanese.

1934 Made trip around the world visiting the Far East, Russia, and Europe.

1935 Killed with famous aviator Wiley Post August 15 in an airplane accident near Point Barrow, Alaska.

CHAPTER 1

Formative Influences

THE story of Will Rogers and his evolution from a cowboy of Oklahoma into a world famous humorist-philosopher is a phenomenon peculiarly American. There is an almost Horatio Alger-like element in the metamorphosis of the cowboy into a vaudeville performer, thence to a nationally known columnist, lecturer, and motion picture actor, and finally to an internationally known humorist who spoke on the events of his time to forty million Americans of all walks of life. To the people of his generation, Will Rogers was the symbol of that abstract concept, "the average man," the "voice of the people" in person; for his gift of humor, which was not average, enabled him to express in words and in a humorous fashion the thoughts, feelings, and attitudes of most Americans about politics, religion, morality, and international affairs. To trace the development of his humor, one must begin first with his ancestry.

Will's story begins appropriately enough with his father, Clem Vann Rogers, a quarter-blood Cherokee Indian, who was born on January 11, 1839, in the Going Snake district of the Cherokee Nation. The father of the future humorist operated a successful trading post in the territory, and in 1859 he wooed and won Mary American Schrimsher, also a quarter-blood Cherokee. Their life together, however, was soon interrupted by the Civil War. Although sympathy in the war was divided among the Cherokees, Clem Vann Rogers joined the Southern Cherokee group and enlisted in the Mounted Cherokee Volunteers under the command of General Stand Watie. As a member of this Confederate regiment, he served with distinction until the end of the war.

When the terms of the surrender compelled the Cherokees to return to Indian Territory, Clem brought his family to the Coo-wee-scoo-wee district; and settled on a homestead allotment on the banks of the Verdigris River, three miles east of the town of Oologah.

Here he turned to ranching and farming, and built a large ranch house for his family. In this house Will Rogers was born on November 4, 1879, the youngest of eight children, only four of whom reached adulthood. He was named Colonel William Penn Adair Rogers in honor of his father's former commanding officer, William Penn Adair, a prominent leader of the Cherokee Nation.[1]

Will was a quarter blood-Cherokee Indian and was so listed in the final census of the Five Civilized Tribes made by the Department of Interior in 1906. He was justly proud of his Cherokee ancestry, for the Cherokees were among the most advanced Indian tribes in North America; they possessed a written alphabet, developed by their great teacher, Sequoyah; and they were the only Indians to publish a newspaper in their own language. Will's paternal grandfather, Robert Rogers, had been a member of the Eastern Cherokees who had moved to Indian Territory shortly before the government's decree in 1835 which had forced all Cherokees to move from their original home in Georgia to a western reservation. The forced move in the winter of 1837-38, known among the Cherokees as the "Trail of Tears," located the Nation on the western border of Arkansas and in the northeast corner of the present state of Oklahoma.

Although not much is known about Will's early life, it seems likely that he was reared like any boy in the territory. He learned to ride a horse almost as soon as he could walk and, as a boy, was taught the skills of a cowboy. His friends were ranchers' sons, and no doubt the activities of the boys reflected the cowboys' work on the range: riding and breaking horses, roping and branding cattle, mending and replacing worn fences, weaning and nursing "dogies."

Will never absorbed much formal education despite the efforts of his mother and father. He first attended the Drumgoole School near Chelsea, a Cherokee institution supported by taxes paid by the members of the Cherokee Nation. After a year, however, his mother decided to send him to the Harrell Institute in Muskogee, which was operated by the Methodist Episcopal Church South. After his mother's death in 1890, Clem Rogers sent his son to the Presbyterian Mission school at Tahlequah, where he stayed one term. In 1892 young Rogers was enrolled in the Willie Halsell School in Vinita, an institution endowed by the Methodist Church South. In his four years at the Halsell School, Will studied reading, writing, history, and art.

In 1895, Clem, who decided that his son was ready for more advanced study, sent him to Scarlitt College in Neosho, Missouri, where the young cowboy spent the next two years. His final formal education was at the Kemper Military Academy, Boonville, Missouri, where, in addition to basic subjects, he studied letter writing, elocution, and geography. In the spring of 1898, Will ran away from Kemper, and never again attended school. Although Will later remarked that he never got beyond the fourth grade, the truth is that he attended school for almost ten years, about the average term of education for boys in Indian Territory. He had learned to read and write and had studied English, history, mathematics, geography, and elocution.

Although Will's interests during the formative years were largely centered around ranching, he was particularly interested in what might be called the peripheral arts of the cowboy — trick riding and fancy roping. The normal jobs of western life — herding cattle, branding calves, hauling feed, repairing fences — he could and did do effectively. But more than anything, he enjoyed the rodeos, where cowboys exhibited their skill in bulldogging steers, riding wild horses, and doing fancy tricks with a lariat. He built up a repertoire of tricks and was as assiduous in practicing them as he was in avoiding school.

Bounded by Claremore, Oologah and Chelsea, his home area was part of the last frontier of America. The country was wild and dangerous not only because of the Indians but also because of rascally white men. The towns were settled, it is true, and substantial citizens lived in them. But, following the Civil War, the Cherokee Nation was flooded with drifters from the North and South who formed an unstable element that was constantly at odds with the respectable citizens. Men wore guns and used them; murder, robbery, and rustling were common crimes in the territory despite the efforts of peace officers sent by the federal government. The Cherokee Nation was the area in which the notorious Dalton gang operated, and its ill-fated raid on a Coffeyville bank in 1883 occurred just fifty-five miles north of Oologah. Cherokee Bill, one of the most notorious desperados of the territory, was hanged in 1884 for a murder committed in Lenapah, just sixteen miles from Oologah. Will was nearly fourteen years old at the time these events happened. All in all, the Cherokee Nation was a land of restlessness, of high spirits, and of violence.

Such rough frontier life is highly conducive to the development of democracy since a man was judged in the territory by his merit as a man, not by his money or his social position. Part of the irreverence which Will later displayed as a humorist reflects the democratic leveling of the frontier, as well as the tendency that marks the American humorist tradition. Because he was reared in the ranch country, he learned early to despise sham and affectation. His admiration and respect went to the cowboys who could rope and throw a steer, not to the ranchers who hired them.

When Will was eighteen, he developed a wanderlust which remained with him the rest of his life. In the spring of 1898, he ran away from school and worked on a ranch in Texas, making a cattle drive up to western Kansas with a herd of longhorns. The following year he traveled to San Francisco and New York City. Such a desire to travel was not an unnatural feeling in young Rogers; it was characteristic of the cattle country and of the men who lived there. Itchy feet was an occupational disease of the cowboy, and it was not uncommon for him to travel from Texas to Montana, working his way from ranch to ranch, for no other reason than to see new country. Cowboys were habitual drifters, to whom distance was unimportant in a land where labor was scarce and good ranch hands were always in demand.

I *South America and South Africa*

The trip to New York opened Will's eyes to the outside world, creating a desire to see more of it. When he returned home, he found that the Southwest was flooded with stories about ranching opportunities in South America. All of the cowboys in Indian Territory were talking about the Argentine where ranches were bigger, the country was freer, and there were no farmers or barbed wire fences. The appeal was irresistible, and Will was determined to go to South America to seek his fortune. Clem Rogers had given his son a small ranch stocked with cattle in hopes of persuading Will to settle down and become a rancher. Now Will offered the ranch and cattle back to his father in return for funds to make the trip. Reluctantly persuaded, his father took back the ranch, paid his son three thousand dollars for the cattle, and Will began to make plans for the long journey to South America.

Accompanied by Dick Paris, a cowboy friend whose expenses he agreed to pay, Will left Oologah in March, 1902, for New Orleans where he hoped to book passage on a boat to South America. But New Orleans had no boats sailing to the Argentine. Ultimately, travel arrangements required the two young adventurers to travel to

New York and thence to England where regularly scheduled ships traveled from Liverpool to Buenos Aires. The boys spent a week in London before shipping out of Liverpool on a boat which landed them in Buenos Aires on May 5, 1902. Will and Dick spent two months in the ranchero country working sometimes for money, but more often for room and board. Dick tired of the adventure quickly and returned home; but young Rogers, although he found the Argentine less glamorous than he had anticipated, was determined to see more of the world. He complained of the food and the climate, but he always had the cowboy's unquenchable optimism about tomorrow — the next ranch or the next country might be just the place for which he was searching. When a cattle buyer offered him a job on a cattle boat sailing for South Africa, Will promptly accepted. It was another part of the world — and perhaps greener pastures.

In South Africa, Will supported himself by working for the stockmen in the area; he drove mules, tended stock, and broke horses. It was the same kind of work he had done at home on his father's ranch in Indian Territory; and South Africa, following the Boer War, was not unlike the American frontier. It was peopled with a conglomerate mixture of European nationals, the British, the Germans, and the Dutch. Will wandered all through the country, and everywhere he found excitement and high spirits in a rugged country full of rugged men. But young Rogers was rough too. Incredibly strong, tough, and resourceful, as a cowboy had to be, he thrived on the hardships and difficulties that he encountered in his travels.

Later Will wrote about his experiences while breaking horses for the British army:

You know these American and Australian horses killed and crippled more soldiers than the Boers. Why they were Western Broncos that had never been broke and then they expected some of the yeomanry that had never rode anything worse than a 'ansome cab to crawl up in the middle of these old snuffy bronks in a little Pancake saddle. Why it was nothing worse than suicide. When a whole company would get new horse and they would holler "Company Mount," in ten seconds you could see nothing but loose horses and Tommies coming up digging the dirt out of their eyes. They had about as much chance staying on top of some of those renegades as man would have sneezing against a cyclone.[2]

In December, 1902, in Johannesburg, Will joined Texas Jack's Wild West Show as a trick rider and roper. He had always felt a vague desire to be a showman; in the rodeos and roundups back home, he had delighted in showing off his roping tricks before an audience. To be paid for what he loved to do best seemed a grand thing to the young cowpuncher. As a member of the Texas Jack's troupe, he did fancy lassoing of running horses and elaborate rope spinning tricks, including the celebrated "Crinoline" which consisted of starting out with a small spinning loop and gradually playing it out until it was ten to fourteen feet in diameter. Will wrote: "We have the best show in South Africa, about 23 horse and 35 people and only 8 Americans with it. The play is partly a circus act and they play blood-curdling scenes of Western life in America, showing Indians and robbers . . . I am called the Cherokee Kid and do all the roping."[3]

For nine months Will traveled with the show. Audiences were receptive and enthusiastic as the circus traveled throughout South Africa: Johannesburg, Sanderton, Pretoria, Durban, and Capetown. He loved the constant change and movement, and the heady tonic of enthusiastic applause. Despite a small gnawing of homesickness, the young cowboy would never again be content to settle as a rancher in Indian Territory. After a year with Texas Jack, Will decided to come home; but he stopped long enough to play with the Wirth Brothers Circus in Australia and to complete his round-the-world trip by traveling to San Francisco and then to Oologah in the spring of 1904.

II *Vaudeville Days*

At twenty-three, then, Will was a widely traveled young man. More important, he had discovered that his avocation had become his vocation. He had learned that the public would pay to see his tricks, and dreams of a career in vaudeville began to form in his mind. When Colonel Zack Mulhall took a Wild West show to the St. Louis Exposition in April, 1904, young Rogers went along as a trick rider and roper; and the following year he accompanied the Colonel to New York to give an exhibition of riding and trick roping in the Horse Fair at Madison Square Garden. When the Mulhall show closed, Will made a big decision — he decided to stay in New York and try to get into vaudeville.

Vaudeville was in its heyday in New York in 1905, and there was a constant search for new talent and novelty. Singers, dancers, comedians, jugglers, magicians, and acrobats were in abundance. Will reasoned that his act, which, in addition to trick roping, included a rider galloping across the stage on a horse, would be unique to say the least. He plodded from booking office to booking office, but the New York theatrical agents were skeptical. There was no demand for such an act; it had never been done before; the public was not interested.

But Will Rogers persisted, and an agent finally scheduled him in Keith's Union Theater, where he made his debut on June 11, 1905. He shuffled out on the stage with his rope in hand and did a few fancy spinning tricks, and then suddenly a horse with a rider dashed across the stage. The young cowboy threw the rope and caught the running horse. That was all. He did not say a word. But the act caught on, and he got a billing in the Victoria Theater. Part of the appeal, of course, was the public's anticipation of the time when Will might miss or the horse might slip; but the hours of weary practice paid off, for not once during the early days did the act go awry.

Classified in vaudeville jargon as a "dumb act" because he did not speak, Will's performance was basically an exhibition of roping which involved the use of ropes of different weights and lengths for special tricks. He would twirl the ropes into loops and fancy patterns, and he performed many spectacular catches such as throwing two ropes at once, catching the rider with one rope and the horse with the other. But always the act closed with the eye-catching stunt known as the Crinoline. For this trick, Will mounted his horse, twirled the rope over his head, and let it out until the loop reached beyond the stage and over the head of the audience. A difficult trick, it demanded an extraordinary blend of coordination and timing; and Will practiced incessantly to improve his roping skill.

Indirectly, it was the public's indifference to the difficulty of his rope handling that led to Rogers' speaking while on the stage. There are conflicting stories about the actual incident, but all agree that Will spoke on the stage for the first time to explain to his audience about the difficulty of a special trick he was about to perform. He simply took off his hat, scratched his head, and drawled, "I want to call your sho-nuff attention to this little stunt I am going to pull on you, as I am going to throw about two of these ropes at once, catching the horse with one and the rider with another. I don't have any idea I'll get it but here goes."[4]

Will began to talk casually during his act. Having no set monologue, he only made a few remarks, usually timed to coincide with a dropped rope or a timing error. Apparently unaware of his audience, he kept his eyes on his ropes and seemed to be talking to himself. His comments appeared to be casual and offhand as if they had just occurred to him. "Swinging a rope is all right," he would say, "when your neck ain't in it. Then it's hell," or he would drawl, "Out West where I come from they won't let me play with this rope. They think I might hurt myself."[5] Although his conversation was not brilliant, he was developing a style. He had a natural drawl and an engaging manner which was particularly effective in developing intimacy between him and his audience. In short, Will Rogers pleased the public.

The act prospered, and Will had no more trouble with bookings. Within a year, he toured Europe, playing before audiences in Germany, England, and Scotland. The old wanderlust was still in him, but there was even a stronger interest back home — Betty Blake of Rogers, Arkansas. Will had met Betty in 1902, shortly before his trip to South America; and he had corresponded with her since that time. When he returned home in 1904, he had visited her. Now his letters indicated an increasing interest, and in November, 1905, he abruptly returned home and proposed. He overcame Betty's objections to life in vaudeville by describing his present tour with the Orpheum circuit as a honeymoon trip to California; and he promised that, once the tour was finished, they would settle down in Claremore, where his father had offered to provide a home. They were married on November 25, 1905, in Rogers, Arkansas. After the ceremony, Will and his bride returned to New York before the tour of the West. The trip was a tremendous success for the humorist. So attractive was the subsequent offer of the Percy Williams chain of theaters that he gave up his thought of retiring from vaudeville, and even Betty agreed to his acceptance of the new contract.

Little has been written about the influence of Betty Rogers upon Will's development as a humorist; yet it is evident that his marriage changed his pattern of living. Rogers had never paid much attention to his physical surroundings. On tour, he stayed at the usual hotels patronized by vaudeville performers, ate in dingy restaurants, and paid little attention to his associates. Betty Rogers insisted that they stay in the better hotels and eat at respectable restaurants. She relieved Will of many household responsibilities including correspondence with his family; and, after the birth of two children, Will, Jr., in 1911 and Mary in 1913, she persuaded Will to take a house at Amityville, New York, where he would be near the center of show business.

Betty Rogers' influence became more apparent as he became

famous. He had a tremendous respect for his wife's judgment and often used her as a testing ground, submitting his quips and jokes for her approval; and, if she questioned the moral or ethical content, Will would discard whatever she objected to. Will, Jr., remarked that "her dictum was final and her influence was such that a whole daily wire would be scrapped and a new one submitted, if she felt that the first was out of line."[6] However, the censorship of Betty Rogers on Will's writing must be considered in relation to her opportunity for reading his material. Quite obviously, many of Will's columns were written and printed without her prior reviewing of the material since much of the time on his travels he was alone.

III   *Ziegfeld Follies*

Meanwhile, Will began to make a name for himself on Broadway. More and more his audiences reacted to his remarks rather than to his roping tricks. Finally in 1915 he broke into big-time vaudeville where he was engaged by Florenz Ziegfeld to play in the *Midnight Frolics,* on the New Amsterdam Roof; and in 1916, while still playing in *Midnight Frolics,* he was given a place in the Ziegfeld Follies.

Will soon found that current topics of the day, taken from the daily newspapers, were a source of humor; and he discovered that a joke does not have to be tremendously funny if it deals with a timely subject. More and more he began to see that the audience liked the truth, but truth salted with exaggeration. He liked for his hearers to nod approval, or nudge their friends and say, "he's right about that." The *New York Times* described Will in the Follies:

When Will Rogers comes on the stage at the Follies with his jaws loaded with chewing gum and his arms loaded with ropes, he makes you feel sorry for him. You know he is going to get tangled up on the ropes or lose a stroke of his gum. He stands there intent on getting a line or rope around each footlight, or that is how it looks from the other side. If he should miss one of those bulbs, you know he'd never get over it. He begins talking in his Oklahoma drawl, and all the while he is chewing gum and playing with the ropes. When he begins to make the ropes writhe like snakes and strike the bulls-eye time and again with his quaint homely wit, you are as proud of him as if you had done it yourself.[7]

Will always felt that the turning point in his career came in 1916 when President Woodrow Wilson attended the Friars Club Frolic in Baltimore. In New York, the humorist had poked considerable fun at the policies of the Wilson administration toward Germany, and toward the Mexican raids made by General Pershing in pursuit of Pancho Villa, the famous Mexican bandit whose forays across the border were a source of embarrassment to the government. But there was a great difference in making these remarks in New York before a nightclub audience and in making them in Baltimore before the President of the United States. Some years later, Rogers described the show:

My first remark in Baltimore was, "I am kinder nervous here tonight." Now that is not an especially bright remark, and I don't hope to go down in History on the strength of it, but it was so apparent to the audience that I was speaking the truth that they laughed heartily at it. After all, we all love honesty. . . . Now Pershing was in Mexico at the time, and there was a lot in the Papers for and against the invasion. I said "I see where they have captured Villa. Yes, they got him in the morning Editions and the Afternoon ones let him get away." Now everybody in the house before they would laugh looked at the President, to see how he was going to take it. Well, he started laughing and they all followed suit. "Villa raided Columbus, New Mexico. We had a man on guard that night at the Post. But to show you how crooked this Villa is, he sneaked up on the opposite side." "We chased him over the line 5 miles, but run into a lot of Government Red Tape and had to come back." "There is some talk of getting a Machine Gun if we can borrow one. The one we have now they are using to train our Army with in Plattsburg. If we go to war we will just about have to go to the trouble of getting another Gun."[8]

His success before the President gave the humorist confidence; if he could poke fun at the President of the United States, then he could go after any person or subject he chose. Moreover, he had become a recognized personality in New York. A great many people heard him, and they repeated his quips to others.

In 1919, Will collected some of his jokes to make his first book, *The Cowboy Philosopher on the Peace Conference.* In the fall, he published a second book, *The Cowboy Philosopher on Prohibition.* The humor of the books is rather bold, but not very original; for example, Will wrote, "The terms of the Armistice read like a mortgage but the Peace Treaty sounds like a foreclosure."[9] Many of the remarks were probably humorous when drawled by Will in his inimitable style before an audience, but they sometimes fall flat on the printed page. If much of the humor seems forced, every now and then there is a sparkle of the wit which characterized his later style in the newspapers.

IV *Newspaper Columnist*

In 1924, one of Will's humorous speeches came to the attention of V. V. McNitt, the founder and publisher of the McNaught Newspaper Syndicate. When he asked Rogers to write a series of weekly humorous articles, to be syndicated throughout the country, Will was interested; but, as he had only limited experience in writing, he was not sure that he was capable. He finally agreed to comment on the current topics of the day just as he did in his stage monologues. He wrote his first weekly column on December 31, 1922. In the *New York Times* appeared this notice: "The famous cowboy monologist, Will Rogers, has undertaken to write for this paper a weekly article of humorous comment upon contemporary affairs."[10] Will had finally found the proper medium for the expression of his humor; through his column, he would become an international personality.

The weekly column was a success. His comments on the events of the day, expressing his shrewd native philosophy, had the effect of crystallizing the unspoken thoughts of the common man. His caustic criticism of government policy, his ironic jabs at Congress, his satiric slants at world disarmament plans, and his realistic appraisal of the motives and methods of American businessmen seemed to confirm for the average man what he had known but could not clearly articulate. His reading audience delighted in his common-sense approach to issues of importance, and they chuckled appreciatively as he deflated the pompous and jeered at the self-righteous. The cowboy humorist appeared to his audience as a typical American: he was a man in suspenders and stocking feet, unpretending and unknowing about these newfangled ideas; but he disposed of them by an application of that great American remedy — common sense.

His daily column came about as a result of his own efforts. While in Europe in the summer of 1926, the humorist wired a telegram to the *New York Times* offering to send a daily telegram of his impressions of Europe if the *Times* would pay the toll. The newspaper accepted the offer, and thus began the daily wire which became a prominent outlet for Will's humor. Usually about a hundred words in length, the daily wire featured Will's penetrating and often sagacious insights about the events of the day. Will received no remuneration for the daily wire until he returned from Europe in October, 1926. On that date the *Times* arranged to buy the feature from the McNaught syndicate which offered the column on a syndicated basis to newspapers throughout the United States.[11]

In 1925, Will went on the lecture platform. Since his monologue in the Follies seldom lasted more than ten minutes, he was at first skeptical about his ability to hold the interest of an audience's attention for a sustained period of time; but he soon found that the lecture platform was a medium perfectly suitable for him. Like Mark Twain before him, nature had equipped him to be a public humorist on the stage. Before an audience he was irresistible. His Oklahoma drawl was peculiarly effective. When Will Rogers walked out on the stage, a shock of hair falling over his forehead, hands in his pockets, and his jaws rhythmically chewing gum, his audience saw in him the exact personality they had read and heard about. He looked his part and acted it unconsciously. His first lecture tour was a tremendous success, and the lecture platform became another outlet for his wit and wisdom.

Will broadened his horizon considerably in 1926 when he traveled to Europe for the *Saturday Evening Post*. He described his impressions of Europe in a series of articles, later published in a book, *Letters of a Self Made Diplomat to His President*. The trip was a real adventure for the developing humorist. He visited England, France, Italy, Switzerland, Spain, and Russia. In England, he met Lady Nancy Astor who introduced him to Sir James Barrie and George Bernard Shaw. He renewed his friendship with the Prince of Wales and spent an evening in the company of such distinguished Englishmen as Sir Harry Lauder, Sir Thomas Lipton, Lord Dewar, Lord Derby, G. K. Chesterton, and Michael Arlen. In Spain, he had tea with the Duke of Alba who introduced him to King Alphonso of Spain. In Italy, he interviewed Mussolini. In Russia, he had little luck in his attempts to meet the Soviet leaders, but his observations about Russia were published in a book, *There's Not a Bathing Suit in Russia*.

Will traveled to other parts of the world as an "unofficial ambassador" of the United States. At the request of Ambassador Dwight Morrow, he traveled to Mexico to accompany the Ambassador and President Calles on an inspection tour of the country. In 1932, at the time of the Manchurian conflict, Will traveled through the Far East visiting Japan, China, and Manchuria. He also visited and lectured in Nicaragua, Panama, and the Philippine Islands. Although Will enjoyed traveling, his visits to the other countries of the world only served to confirm his belief that the United States was the greatest country on earth, and he was always glad to get home again. Despite his travels throughout the world, the humorist remained a provincial American; although he was conscious of the shortcomings of democracy, he still maintained an unashamed pride in American institutions.

One factor which undoubtedly contributed to the development of Will's humor was the fact that he was forty-two years of age when he began to write his column. He had outgrown the normally rebellious nature of the twenty- and thirty-year olds, and he had also mellowed considerably before he began to write. Whatever fires of reform or righteous zeal had once burned in him had turned to ashes by the time he became an author. He displayed anger or irritation at times at what he regarded as ill-advised or foolish actions which affected the nation; but, since he felt that his proper sphere was humor rather than reform, he never struck quite so hard or so bitterly at the foibles of human nature as Finley Peter Dunne or as Mark Twain had done before him.

V *Motion Pictures and Radio*

Meanwhile, two other mediums of expression for his humor opened for Will: motion pictures and the radio. As early as 1919, he had made a motion picture for Samuel Goldwyn. On the silent screen he played in such movies as *Laughing Bill Hyde, Jubilo,* and *The Roping Fool,* none of which was a notable success, and Will returned to New York and the Follies. Then in 1929, he made his first talking picture, *They Had to See Paris,* which was a tremendous success; and his subsequent pictures established him as one of the foremost attractions in the movie industry. In such films as *A Connecticut Yankee in King Arthur's Court, See America First, Life Begins at Forty,* and *Steamboat 'Round the Bend,* Will entertained audiences, who, having read his columns, could now see him on the screen. Generally, his roles required him to play characters who displayed simple human emotions with sincerity and conviction, and he seldom disappointed his admirers.

In 1926, Will made his first radio broadcast, later signing a contract for a weekly radio appearance. The magic of his personality was just as effective over the radio as on the platform, and millions of Americans listened to his programs each week.

It was in his syndicated newspaper column, however, that Will developed his reputation as a humorist. He often said, "All I know is what I read in the papers," and he read several newspapers every day searching for a humorous slant to the news. He read not only the news and editorials but also the financial and sports sections, the feature stories, and the columnists. He read Walter Lippmann, O. O. McIntyre, H. L. Mencken, Arthur Brisbane, and Dr. Harry Emerson Fosdick. He must have read Mr. Dooley, for Finley Peter Dunne published his column as late as 1927. It was Rogers' custom, according to his sons, to read several newspapers each evening before retiring and to read several morning editions on the following day.[12]

It is hard to estimate the influence of books on Will's humor. According to Will, Jr., his father read most of the American humorists, particularly his contemporaries such as Ring Lardner, Irving S. Cobb, George Ade, and Kin Hubbard. He was an admirer of Mark Twain, and his favorite book was *Life on the Mississippi*, which he kept on a table by his bedside. He was apt to read contemporary authors recommended to him by such friends as Henry L. Mencken and Will Durant. Will also read some of the plays of George Bernard Shaw and some novels by James Barrie before interviewing these writers in London in 1926; later in his column the humorist commented favorably on Shaw's critical work. There are frequent references to Shakespeare in Rogers' columns, but he probably learned his Shakespeare from the theater rather than from his reading. James Rogers, the humorist's youngest son, remembered that his father did a great deal of reading at home; but he could recall only two specific authors, Bret Harte and Rudyard Kipling. James also said that his father spent a great deal of time reading movie scenarios which his producers sent him. All in all, demands upon Will's time prevented him from reading as widely as he might have liked.[13]

Will Rogers shared a characteristic with Mark Twain: he liked to keep on the move. It is virtually impossible to keep track of his journeying. He traveled around the world three times, and he visited every country in the world with the exception of parts of Africa. He made additional trips to Europe, spending considerable time in France, England, Germany, Italy, Spain, and Russia. He toured South America, visiting nations on both the Atlantic and Pacific sides. His lecture tours took him everywhere in the United States. There was a restlessness in his heart that made him want to go everywhere and see everything. He was killed on his last great adventure, when the plane in which he and Wiley Post were flying across the top of the world to Russia crashed on August 15, 1935, at Point Barrow, Alaska.

It was ironic that Will should lose his life in an airplane accident. For years he had flown everywhere in the United States and in Europe, always advocating the safety of flight in modern airplanes with trained pilots at the controls. In those days of aviation's infancy, he constantly reiterated his belief in the future of aviation; and he backed up his words by flying whenever that form of transportation was available to him. He knew all of the famous pilots of the pioneer days of aviation: he was a friend and defender of General Billy Mitchell whose efforts to develop an army air force were defeated by an economy-minded Congress and conservative army staff; he flew with Charles Lindbergh in Mexico and with the speed king, Frank Hawks, on a charity tour of the Midwest on behalf of the victims of the Mississippi flood in 1932. His companion on the final trip was Wiley Post, a fellow Oklahoman and one of the early heroes of aviation, who only a year before had set a record for a flight around the world.

The purpose of the final flight was to survey the possibilities of a mail-passenger air route from the United States to Russia which would avoid the hazards of the long flight over the Pacific ocean. Will had never visited Alaska or Siberia, and the idea of a new adventure fascinated him. On August 8, he joined Post in Seattle, and the pair took off for Juneau, Alaska, where Will visited with an old friend, Rex Beach, the western novelist. They then flew on to Anchorage and Fairbanks, where Will filed his last daily wire on August 15. The next stop was to be Point Barrow, Alaska, the farthest point of land on the American continent — but the plane never made it. A lone Eskimo fisherman, Clare Okpeaha, was the only witness of the tragedy; and his report to Sergeant Stanley R. Morgan of the United States Signal Corps in Point Barrow was recorded as follows by Alaskan newspapers:

En route to the scene of the accident, Sergeant Morgan quizzed Okpeaha in an effort to learn more. Asked as to how he knew there were two men in the plane, Okpeaha replied, "Me talk with mans."

Sergeant Morgan said, "When? After they fell?"

"No," answered Okpeaha, "when they came down on water and asked me how go Barrow, where Barrow is, how far."

"Did they tell you their names?"

"No," replied Okpeaha, "mans no tell name. But big mans. One man sore eye. He go inside plane and mans with sore eye start engine and go up. Engine spit, start, then stop. Start some more little. Then plane fall just so."

And with his hands Okpeaha indicated a bank, a fall on the right wing, a nose dive in the water, followed by a complete somersault.

When Sergeant Morgan asked if he waded out to the plane after the crash, Okpeaha said, "No me stand on sandspit, forty feet away, and holler to mans. No answer, and so me hurry quick to Barrow to tell people come quick."[14]

Not since Mark Twain had any humorist been so beloved by the American people; and, in the years following his death, Will Rogers became a legend. He became apotheosized as the average American who represented the very best of American life. The humorist earned this position in the hearts of his countrymen by writing his observations of his age in the guise of a homely, crackerbox sage whose common-sense pronouncements reflected the pattern of American thought in the 1920's. Consequently, Will Rogers deserves consideration not only in the history of his time but in the literature of humor as well.

CHAPTER 2

Apprenticeship Days

TO understand the development of the vaudeville comedian into a shrewd and penetrating political commentator, one must begin with Will Rogers' early career when he was developing his techniques of humor. During his first few years in show business, he thought of himself as primarily a trick-rope artist, demonstrating an incredible agility and dexterity in handling a lariat. He had no thoughts of becoming a humorist; and, when he spoke for the first time on the stage to explain the difficulty of a roping trick he was about to perform, he was outraged at the laughter which greeted his remarks. His first impulse was to believe that the laughter indicated a lack of appreciation for his roping skill.

However, Will soon recognized that the audience had laughed with him, not at him; and he began to add impromptu jokes about his roping tricks to his routine. As audience appreciation mounted, he expanded his remarks; he commented on the performers who had preceded him on the bill, he joshed and joked about the conditions in the theater, and he sometimes roped unsuspecting stagehands in the wings, where they had gathered to watch his act. Throughout his routine, Will made his comments without looking at his audience, thus giving the impression that his jokes were original and spontaneous, ideas that had just suddenly occurred to him on the stage.

Actually, Will's humorous remarks were not so casual and offhand as they appeared to be. He had a natural, quick wit and was capable of improvising humorous remarks for unexpected situations which sometimes developed in his roping act. Yet, once he was convinced of the value of humor to his act, he worked long and hard in developing a set of jokes which would cover virtually every situation. In the Will Rogers Memorial at Claremore, Oklahoma, there is a wrinkled piece of stationery from the Saratoga Hotel in Chicago on which Will had written several jokes that he later used in his routine as the occasion demanded. Labeled "Gags for Missing the Horses Nose," these jokes are indicative of Will's early humor:

1. I think I will turn him around and see if I can throw one on his tail.
2. If I dont get one pretty soon, I will have to give out rain checks.
3. Hi you Jasper, I think I will see if I cant get just one on your nose, if it dont make any difference to you out there.
4. If I have a whole bunch of good luck, I will get this one on about the 13th throw if this salary wing dont give out on me.
5. I should of sprinkled a little musilage on his nose, this thing might then hang on.
6. There is hope. Well, we are all chock full of hope. If there was a little better roping and less hoping, we would get out of here earlier tonight.
7. This is easier to do on a blind horse, they dont see the rope coming.[1]

During his first five years in show business, Will was never a headliner, but he was seldom without booking dates. His roping skills and his humorous remarks carried him throughout the country on the Orpheum circuit. He secured the services of an agent who booked him into the biggest theatrical houses in New York where he gradually built for himself a reputation as a humorist.

In 1910, Will discarded the horse roping portion of his act and developed a new routine which was basically a humorous monologue attended by a variety of roping tricks. In expanding his material, he tried a variety of humorous devices, including the telling of jokes in the manner of a vaudeville comedian. But he soon found that this form of humor was not suitable for him. His best success came from the comments which he himself made up out of his own observations and experience. His act was thus distinctive for its originality and spontaneity.

Richard Henry Little, critic for the *Chicago Tribune,* reviewed Will's act in 1911:

Will Rogers, the Oklahoma cowboy, was one of the most pronounced hits on the program. The accomplished Mr. Rogers not only delights the audience with his amazing dexterity with his lasso, but even more with his running fire of small talk. The great beauty of Mr. Rogers' conversation is that he never is quite through with what he has to say. He makes a remark, and apparently marks a period by doing some impossible-looking rope trick with the lasso, and that portion of his audience that sympathizes with his statement applauds wildly. The inconsistent Mr. Rogers drops another drawling remark that is diametrically opposed to the first statement, and starts another section of the crowd to clapping wildly. Then as this second tumult dies away, he makes still another comment along the line of the original thought that is a bit more pertinent than either of the first two, and may differ widely from both.[2]

As Will matured as a humorist, he began to seek other outlets for his talent. In the next few years he appeared in three Broadway shows, *The Wall Street Girl, Hands Off,* and *Ned Wayburn's Town Topics.* Although none of these productions ran for any length of time, Will received good critical reviews for his part in them. In 1915, Will attracted the attention of Gene Buck, a writer for Florenz Ziegfeld, the producer of the famous Follies. At this time, Ziegfeld had a second production, *The Midnight Frolics,* which began at the stroke of midnight on the New Amsterdam Roof. The *Frolics* was a kind of glorified night club where food and drink were served, and the entertainment was largely furnished by beautiful girls from the Follies. Buck persuaded Ziegfeld to book Will Rogers into the *Frolics* as a humorous foil to the girls who were Ziegfeld's trademark.

I *Comedian to Humorist*

Will survived the first few weeks in the *Frolics,* but not without difficulty. The monologue which had served him well in vaudeville could not sustain him in the new show where the audience generally averaged about fifty percent "repeaters" each evening. New material had to be developed when his jokes and gags began to fall flat before a sophisticated audience that expected new entertainment daily. Faced with the necessity of changing his material for every show, Will strained to develop new material; but interest in his act began to lag, and, although Will did not know it, he was in danger of being released from the *Frolics.*

Then, at the suggestion of Betty, his wife, he turned to contemporary events and topical news which he found in the daily newspapers. Henceforth, he would be a topical humorist dealing with current events and personalities. He would become an interpreter of the news, depending on his native wit and shrewd insight to find a humorous angle to all items of public interest. The first night that he began to talk about what he had read in the newspapers, the "new" Will Rogers was an instant success. He was so successful, in fact, that within a year, Ziegfeld had placed him in the Follies which meant that the humorist had to prepare a monologue for two matinees and two evening performances each day. Such activity put a strain upon him for material, but, Will explained,

I get my jokes out of the newspapers, not out of the funny columns, but out of the latest news. At the matinee I pull stuff based on the noon editions of the afternoon papers. Well, before the evening performance all the matinee stuff is stale for the audience, so I use the sporting editions, finals and home issues. But by the time the *Midnight Frolics* starts, these late evening jokes are also stale, so I get the first edition of the *Morning Telegraph* and make my monologue out of that. I buy more newspaper extras than any man in the world because I've made up my mind no joke goes over after it is six hours old.[3]

Will's typical Follies patter, according to Donald Day, ran something like this:

Bryan is against every public issue that comes up. . . . About the only thing he is pleased with is himself. . . . When Ford's peace ship sailed I went over to see it off. . . . I got there just in time to hear Bryan say, "God bless you." . . . Thats the only thing he says for nothing. . . . Well you have to give him credit. . . . He held out for more money . . . I thought for a while it might be a success. . . . Bryan didn't go. . . . President Wilson says a man has a right to change his mind and should, but Bryan has been doing the same act for 14 years. . . . Bryan is really in earnest about preparedness. . . . He is going to make a few free talks on it. . . .[4]

With Will's commitment to the newspapers as a source for his humor, he found plenty to talk about. News in 1916 was both plentiful and exciting; it was the second winter of World War I and the third year of President Wilson's administration. The humorist avidly read the newspapers, and each evening at the Follies he ambled out on the stage before his audience, grinning and chewing gum: "All I know is what I read in the newspapers," he would begin; then shrewd and telling comments poured forth from his lips in an apparently casual fashion. The *New York Times* reviewed his act in 1916:

Now Mr. Rogers is nothing if not individual; he is also American from the grass roots — the most American of present day comedians, in fact, since through his veins there courses authentic Cherokee Indian blood. . . . When he slouches out onto the stage grinning and savagely chewing gum, while intermittently giving his nose a furtive rub with the back of his hand, he is *not* acting — he is merely being himself. And the things he says are *not* the jokes of some writer, retained to supply him with fresh material, but his own individual observations on the ever-amusing human comedy about us. . . . Mr. Rogers' act which forms the most intellectual part of the Follies, is the product of many years of hard work. His sense of satire, which seeks out the very weakest links in every chain of words, is a genuine gift. . . .[5]

Actually Will's humor had not greatly changed since his days in vaudeville. He still used the same mannerisms, talked in the same Oklahoma drawl, and gave the same appearance of speaking in a casual manner. But he had refined these techniques and had made them just as much his trademark as his twirling ropes and chewing gum. He had also learned two important lessons about humor which would serve him for the rest of his career. He had learned, first, that the timely element of a joke is often the secret of its success; he became aware that a joke does not have to be uproariously funny if it deals with a timely subject. And, second, he learned that prominent men, personalities in the news, like to be kidded and satirized, provided either is done in the spirit of fun with no malice intended.

By 1919, Will's comments in the Follies centered on two of the most important topics of the day, the Versailles Conference and prohibition. The Versailles Conference, which marked the end of World War I, had been in the news for months. Most people in the United States were confused by the conflicting areas of interest which developed among the Allies following the war. President Wilson had gone to the conference, carrying with him his Fourteen Points, which presumably would form the basis for a just settlement and a lasting peace. But the viewpoints of England, France, Italy, and other Allied nations did not coincide with those of the President; for these countries wanted to impose severe punishment upon Germany and to demand large reparations for the damage suffered during the war. As the conference progressed, Will began making jokes about it; and so successful were his comments that in July, 1919, he collected some of his material and published his first book, *The Cowboy Philosopher on the Peace Conference.*

II *Apprenticeship Writing*

Although Will Rogers had been a successful humorist on the vaudeville platform for fourteen years, this book was his first attempt at humorous writing. In an effort to project his stage personality on the printed page, he leaned heavily on ludicrous spellings and expressions, just as many American humorists before him had done. As to content, Will's humor in his first book centered largely on the diplomatic maneuvers of President Wilson and the American delegation at the conference. The humorist was a strong admirer of the President, and most of his quips are based upon President Wilson's experience in Europe. For example, he remarked: "President Wilson played a whole week of one night stands in Italy. He carried a letter of introduction from Enrico Caruso so he naturally was able to meet some of the best people in all of Italy."[6] The inference that Caruso, the great Italian tenor, could provide an entree to the better class of people for the President of the United States is the kind of incongruity that amused Rogers' audiences.

Will had a lot of fun with the names of Europeans. The Russians became the "Rooshians" and the Hungarians were the "Hungeriuns." As to Czechoslovakia, he wrote: "Now the Pres says that we are going to recognize them Checho-Slovaks we may recognize them But I am dead sure that we will never Pronounce them."[7] When difficulties over the German war debt to the Allies developed at the conference, Will wrote: "Everybody around the Table wants a second helping and Germany the Cook hasent got ENOUGH to go around. They agree on ONE of the 14 points. That was that America went into this war for NOTHING, she expects NOTHING, so they are unanimous that she gets NOTHING."[8] As to the Fiume-Trieste dispute, he said, "Italy says if they don't get Fiume they will pick up their marbles and go home. Pres Wilson says you may Fiume but you will never get it."[9]

As the conference continued into its third month, it became apparent that Wilson's efforts to establish peace on the basis of his Fourteen Points were doomed to failure. However, the President had made it clear for some time that he considered the establishment of a League of Nations as the most important function of the Peace Conference — so important that he was willing to sacrifice everything else to obtain it. Will wrote, "Pres Wilson wanted to put the LEAGUE OF NATIONS in with the Peace Treaty. Thats about like a Fellow going into a store and the Merchant wont sell him a suit unless he uses a Gillette razor . . . Best time to have formed this here League of Nations was DURING THE WAR when all these Nations NEEDED each other so bad. . . . One thing about this League, in the last War there was only 10 or 15 nations in it. Now if they all sign this Thing they can ALL be in the next ONE, it wont be near so EXCLUSIVE."[10]

When the final terms of the Treaty of Versailles were announced, Will, like many other Americans, was surprised at the severity of the provisions. The immensity of the reparation settlements and the territorial seizures seemed to be inconsistent with the Wilsonian philosophy of a just peace. Will wrote, "I had an idea that these Armistace terms READ like a Second Mortgage, But this Document reads like it was a FORECLOSURE." But he added, "But of course my real SENTIMENTS ARE THE SAME as everybody else — ANYTHING TO PREVENT WAR."[11]

Encouraged by the success of his first book, which went through two printings for a total of six thousand copies, the humorist collected some of his jokes about Prohibition and published a second volume in August, 1919, entitled, *The Cowboy Philosopher on Prohibition.* Since Prohibition was one of the highly controversial topics of postwar America, Will found it a rich source of humor. Although the restrictive law was too new to be properly evaluated, he early recognized its most apparent weakness; he foresaw that many Americans would regard the Volstead Enforcement Act as an invasion of personal privacy and would not consider this law on the same basis as statutes about such crimes as robbery or arson. They would not feel under obligation to report violators of the act, nor would they vote for city officials who would strictly enforce it.

Will Rogers, like many Americans, felt that beer and light wine did not constitute intoxicating beverages. Although Will himself did not drink, he had little sympathy for any attempt to legislate against personal habits of others. Consequently, the ardent Prohibitionists became the butt of many of his jokes in his Follies routine. He defined a Prohibitionist, for example, as "a Man or Woman, who is so satisfied with himself that he presents himself with the 'Croix de perfect He.' He gives himself this Medal because he is now going to start to Meddle in Everybodies business but his own."[12] His definition was obviously designed to suit his sophisticated New York audience, but the humorist himself felt that the Prohibitionists had exaggerated considerably the evils of drinking. With the Bible as a text, they constantly pointed to scripture verse which supported their position. In a kind of burlesque, Will joked at the scripture evidence: "The PROHIBITIONISTS rave about water. Now old Noah knew more about water than all the rest of them put together. In fact he was the FIRST WATER COMMISSIONER of his time. He was a real expert on water, and the very first man smart enough NOT TO

DRINK IT. He was also the first one to find some use for it, you could float a BOAT ON IT, but as a beverage it was a washout."[13]

Will's first two books show definite traces of his vaudeville technique. Since his quips are treated as separate jokes, there is no continuity in the writing. Some of them seem weak on the printed page, although they were successful when delivered on the stage in an Oklahoma drawl. Much of the material seems strained, as if he had been forced to extend a short quip to a paragraph to suit the requirements of a book. That basic truths are found in many of the comments indicates the shrewd and practical mind of the cowboy-humorist. Moreover, his remarks were fundamentally in agreement with the thinking of the majority of Americans about the peace treaty and Prohibition. As a reviewer of the second book observed, "There are very few of those serious points that have been knots to the public mind that he does not unravel with his light-hearted philosophy."[14]

As a result of Will's success in the Follies, he found other fields of entertainment opening for him. Samuel Goldwyn offered him a part in the movie, *Laughing Bill Hyde;* and, on the strength of his performance, Will was offered a contract to make movies in Hollywood at twice the salary which Ziegfeld paid him. But his initial experience in the movies was not a happy one; for, despite a modest success as an actor over a two-year period, Will's contract was not renewed when Goldwyn sold his operation to become part of the newly formed Metro-Goldwyn-Mayer corporation. Chagrined and not a little humiliated, Will decided to become his own producer and actually filmed three one-reel pictures: *Fruits of Faith, One Day in 365,* and *The Roping Fool.* Unfortunately, the business complexities involved in producing movies were overwhelming, and Will soon found himself so deeply in debt that he had to mortgage his home and sell his Liberty Bonds to satisfy his creditors. He returned to New York to recoup his financial losses.

Although he was able to return to the Follies, Will's need for additional income to pay his debts was so great that he asked his agent to book him for after-dinner speaking engagements throughout the New York area. His reputation was such that he was able to command a sizable fee for speaking to such organizations as the National Association of Manufacturers, the Automobile Manufacturers, the Chamber of Commerce, and a host of others. He called such a performance "barking for my dinner," and he did it so well that he averaged almost four speeches a week for a year after his return from California.

His after-dinner speeches were modeled on his Follies routine: he employed the same mannerisms, the same slow-speaking drawl, and the same sharp wit. His opening remark was always an attention-arresting insult which was embellished with illustrations and anecdotes and which was delivered in a disarming, humorous fashion which seemed to suggest that all was in fun. In a speech to the International Bankers Association in 1922, he said:

Loan Sharks and Interest Hounds, I have addressed every form of organized Graft in the U.S. excepting Congress. So its naturally a pleasure for me to appear before the biggest. You are without doubt the most disgustingly rich audience I ever talked to, with the possible exception of the Bootleggers Union Local No 1 combined with enforcement officers. . . . I see where your Convention was opened by a Prayer, and you had to send outside your ranks to get somebody that could pray. You should have had one Creditor there, he would have shown you how to pray. I noticed that in the prayer, the Clergyman announced to the Almighty that the Bankers were here. Well it wasent exactly an announcement, It was more in the nature of a warning. . . . You have a wonderful organization, I understand you have 10 thousand here and with what you have in the various Federal Prisons brings your membership up to around 30 thousand. So Goodby Paupers, You are the finest bunch of Shylocks that ever forclosed a Mortgage on a Widows home.[15]

On October 26, 1922, Will made his first political speech in support of Ogden L. Mill who was seeking reelection to Congress. When Will rose before the audience, he announced that he did not know the candidate, did not want to know the candidate, but could probably find something favorable to say about him. "His handicap is that he was educated at Harvard. But I understand he has forgotten most of it, so that brings him back to earth. . . . He is the only Politician outside Henry Cabot Lodge that can get into the front door of a Fifth Avenue Home without delivering something. . . . He favors a living wage for bootleggers and a free examination for those who drink their products. . . . "[16]

The speech was covered by a reporter of the *New York Times* which printed the entire text the following day. Widely read and discussed, the humorous speech caught the attention of V.V. McNitt, founder and owner of the McNaught Newspaper Syndicate. Impressed by the speech and sensing the market potential of a humorous political column, McNitt offered Will a contract to write a weekly series of humorous articles to be syndicated in newspapers throughout the country. In December, 1922, Will made his debut as a weekly columnist; under the contract with the McNaught syndicate, he was to produce a Sunday feature on his observations of the news of the day. Four years later, in October, 1926, he signed another contract with McNaught to produce a daily column, one much shorter in length, to be syndicated throughout the United States. At the time of his death in 1935, around three hundred fifty daily papers and two hundred Sunday papers were carrying his column to approximately forty million readers.

When Will became a columnist in 1922, the total amount of his written work was two small volumes of humor, which ran, together, to little over a hundred pages and a few miscellaneous articles for the newspapers. As a newspaper columnist, whose beat was the world, he was now responsible for producing a weekly article of approximately twenty-five hundred words in a humorous tone about contemporary events. Employing the same ungrammatical style which characterized his first attempts at public writing, he now described for his readers his reactions to, and observations on, the news of the day, commenting on policies and issues, public figures and personalities of both national and international importance. There were, in fact, few items of newsworthy significance which the humorist did not touch on in his column.

CHAPTER 3

Observer of His Age:
The National Scene

THE approach to the humor of Will Rogers lies first in an understanding of his era. World War I had been followed, as all wars are, by a period of unrest, emptiness, and disillusionment. The decade was disjointed by extremist ideologies: a wave of aggressive nationalism, right-wing hysteria over the threat of Socialism, racial intolerance and anti-intellectualism were manifestations of the popular mind in postwar America. Many of the young generation of Americans in the 1920's thought of themselves as a "lost generation" adrift in a world of disintegrating values, and their manner of living was a distinct rebellion against the standards of their elders. Thus the 1920's became an era of extremes: the Harding scandals, Charles Lindbergh's flight to Paris, Aimee Semple McPherson, Al Capone, Prohibition and speakeasies, and unparalleled prosperity followed by the "big bust." Against this background of the "Jazz Age," Will Rogers satirized and poked fun at the foibles and follies of the inhabitants of what he facetiously referred to as "Cuckooland."

Because Will's humor is so firmly grounded in the events of his time, much of it seems ephemeral. The point of topical humor often finds its frame of reference in the event that inspired it; and, when the topic loses its interest, the humor sometimes fades with it. The humorist was fond of saying, "All I know is what I read in the papers"; and, although such topical humor is extremely effective to those for whom it was written, much of it loses its significance with the passage of time. Artemus Ward, Petroleum V. Nasby, and, to a certain extent, Mr. Dooley suffered from the same effect; the humor they created on topical subjects is still present, but the audience for whom it was written no longer exists, and the events which inspired it are no longer of public interest. Similarly, much of Will's wit may not appear so sharp to modern readers as it did to his contemporaries who were familiar with the events and personalities of the 1920's.

But Will's humor had a unique characteristic: it was based upon his personal philosophy which to a large degree reflected his frontier background and education. His philosophy, based upon truth as Will saw it, concerned the economic, social, moral and political behavior of the American people. His was the kind of philosophy that caused Donald Day, editor of the *Autobiography of Will Rogers,* to write, "When all of Will's writings are published, they will constitute the best *blow by blow* history of a period ever written. . . . For the first time the 'big Honest Majority' will have a history not written by a propagandist or pedant; for the first time the people will have a history written as they would write it if articulate."[1] Rogers' humorous observations do more, therefore, than merely entertain; in a very real way, they often reflect the feelings and attitudes of a generation.

I *Congress and Congressmen*

From Washington Irving's time to the present, Congress and Congressmen have been a source of humor to public commentators. American humorists have long viewed the activities and antics of Congressmen as amusing and sometimes as incomprehensible to their constituents. Since the American people have never held public servants in awe, one of the hazards of a political career in the United States has always been the barbed satire and caustic comments from a free electorate. Indeed, the American voter seems to feel an obligation to speak openly on all government matters which he dislikes or disapproves; and elected representatives have to expect much impudence and some irreverence from the voters.

Early in his career, Will recognized the rich ore of humor to be extracted by prying into the daily activities of the government. He knew that the average citizen had a limited knowledge of the actual machinery of government and was instinctively distrustful of the elaborate, complicated method by which Congress conducted its business through committees, debates, and hearings. Since many American voters thought of Congress purely in terms of party politics, they damned the Democrats or Republicans as the case might be; and they were usually content to ascribe all unpopular legislation to the opposing party.

Will himself was fully aware of the complex problems of the legislature; but, being an apostle of common sense, he preferred that

Congress act in the best interest of the United States. As a result he was heartily opposed to partisanship in government, particularly when it involved blind loyalty to a particular party. Although the humorist himself was a registered Democrat, he never let himself become entangled in party politics.

Will felt that he could ill afford to be associated with either political party if he wished to remain free to examine impartially the political scene. In 1918, Theodore Roosevelt told Albert Lasker, a member of the Republican National Committee, "This fellow, Will Rogers, has such a keen insight into our American panorama and the thinking of our American people that I have a feeling that he is bound, in the course of time, to be a most potent factor in the political life of our country. His goodwill can be an inestimable asset to our party."[2] But apparently any overtures made to him by Republican leaders were turned down, for he never openly supported either party.

Will had a simple criterion: legislation should be judged as right or wrong insofar as it was good or bad for the United States. He wrote:

[Congressmen should] vote on what they thought was good for the Majority of the people of the U.S. That would be a Cinch. But what makes it hard for them is every time a Bill comes up they have a million things to decide that have nothing to do with the merit of the Bill. They first must consider is, or was, it introduced by a member of the opposite Political Party. If it is, why then something is wrong with it from the start, for everything the opposite side does has a catch in it. Then the principal thing is of course, "what will this do for me personally back home?" If it is something that he thinks the folks back home may never read, or hear of, why then he can vote any way he wants to, but Politics and Self-Preservation must come first, never mind the majority of the people of the U.S. If Lawmakers were elected for Life I believe they would do better. A man's thoughts are naturally on his next term, more than on his Country. Outside the Congress Hall, they are as fine a bunch of men as any one ever met in his life. They are full of Humor and regular fellows. That is, as I say, when you catch them when they haven't got Politics on their Minds. But the minute they get in that immense Hall they begin to get Serious, and it's then that they do such Amusing Things. If we could just send the same bunch of men to Washington for the Good of the Nation, and not for Political Reasons, we could have the most perfect Government in the world.[3]

Such expressions on partisan politics reflected Will's independent thinking. As a result, his readers seem to have expected him to challenge and expose any such tendencies in national affairs on the part of Congressmen which he might recognize. He struck devastatingly at the follies of the Democratic spokesmen, and in the next breath he mercilessly derided the pomposity of the Republican leaders. Both parties felt the sting of his ridicule when Congressional action on a piece of legislation showed a strong party bias, for he had no patience for Congressmen who voted "down the line" on any issue:

If Parties are supposed to have to vote together on everything, let each Party only send one man from the entire United States. Why pay these others just to be a lot of sheep. Party politics is the most narrow-minded occupation in the World. A Guy raised in a straight Jacket is a corkscrew compared to a thick-headed Party Politician. All you would have to do to make some men Atheists is just tell them the Lord belongs to the Opposition Political Party. After that they could never see any good in him.[4]

As the *Saturday Review of Literature* reported, "Somebody once gave him a license for free speech (or perhaps he just took it without asking); but at any rate, in the past few years he has probably turned over more heavy stones and thrown hot sunshine upon the poor human grub underneath than any other man in the United States."[5]

Despite his knowledge of the procedures through which Congress operated, Will did not hesitate to condemn practices which seemed to him to be obstructive in nature. He was particularly bitter at the use of a filibuster to prevent a piece of legislation from coming to a vote in the Senate. He wrote:

They are having what is called a Fillibuster in the Senate. The name is just as silly as the thing itself. It means that a man can get up and talk for 15 or 20 years at a time, then he is relieved by another, just to keep some Bill from coming to a vote, no matter about the merit of this particular Bill, whether it is good or bad. The whole foundation of our Government is based on majority rule, so they have done their duty when they merely vote against it or for it, whichever they like. There is no other body of Lawmakers in the world that has a thing like that. Why if a distinguished Foreigner was to be taken to see our Institutions and was taken into the Senate and not told what the Institution was, and heard a man ramble on, talking that had been going on for 10 or 12 hours, he would probably say, "You have lovely quarters for your insane, but have you no Warden to look after their health — to see that they don't talk themselves to death?" . . . One Senator threatened to read the Bible into the record as part of his speech. And I guess he would have done it if somebody in the Capitol had had a Bible. Now that would have been a good thing, for it would have given a lot of them a chance to hear what it says. But, of course, that was even too sensible to go through.[6]

In 1925 a bill was introduced in Congress to raise the pay of Senators and Representatives from $7,500 to $10,000 a year. Will was delighted with Congressional reaction to the bill. Because few members of Congress cared to stand and be counted on this issue, he proposed facetiously that it might be a good economic idea to consider paying the Congressmen exactly what they were worth, a move which might save the country a great deal of money. Such a man as Senator William Borah of Idaho, he noted, might command a princely sum; others might be forced to pack and go home. However, the humorist concluded, "I figure that if we pay 'em good it might encourage them to do better. They do like flattery, and if we raise their pay and sorter kid 'em along they may amount to something yet."[7]

In one respect, the humorist was like Jonathan Swift, who hated and detested the animal called "man" but heartily loved the individual John, Peter, Thomas, and the rest. Will himself had no respect for the professional party politician *per se,* but he had many friends in Congress whom he admired and respected for their service to the United States. Although he visited with government officials, listened to their comments, and occasionally quoted them in his column, he seldom referred to an individual Congressman by name in a derogatory sense.

In 1925 when a Congressman was apprehended bringing liquor into the United States, Rogers omitted the name; but he used the incident to jibe at Congress as a whole:

A bunch of Congressmen landed in New York from the Panama Canal where they had been at government expense to see if it really did connect the two oceans, or was it just propaganda. Well they got back here to New York and they only searched one of their baggage and found four quarts. The other 14 had claimed it and got home with theirs. All but Congressman La Guardia, an Italian American (and a good one). He admitted that he had started from down there with a few steins of grog, but he had drank it up before arrival at Quarantine, purposely. Now he will be ostracized from Congress for honesty.[8]

Will was caustic in his criticism when Congress refused to pass a bill appropriating fifteen million dollars for food relief during the depression. When Congress turned the bill down, he noted that it appropriated the same amount to improve entrances to national parks. "In two years," he remarked, "there won't be a poor farm that don't have a concrete road leading up to it."[9] When Congress failed to pass legislation benefiting the farmer and small businessman, he became incensed. Then on January 6, 1931, a group of five hundred farmers, whose credit was exhausted and whose families were without food, marched into England, Arkansas, and demanded food. Will warned Congress and the administration:

We got powerful Government, brainy men, great organizations, many commissions, but it took a little band of five Hundred simple country people (who had no idea they were doing anything historical) to come to a country town store and demand food for their wives and children. They hit the heart of the American people more than all your senatorial pleas and government investigations. Paul Revere just woke up Concord, these birds woke up America. I don't want to discourage Mr. Mellon and his carefully balanced budget, but you let this country get hungry and they are going to eat, no matter what happens to Budgets, Income Taxes or Wall Street values. Washington mustn't forget who rules when it comes to a showdown.[10]

Where the farmer was concerned, the humorist could be blunt; for he felt that a Congress which worried about a balanced budget when people were going hungry had lost its sense of values. "Congressional oratory on the farm problem," he noted, "may be an organic exercise, but it is a digestive failure."[11] As the *Nation* remarked, "It is just as well for Mr. Rogers that his caustic observations are wrapped in humor. If they were delivered without the funny tags, his audience would set the dogs on him."[12]

When President Franklin Delano Roosevelt was elected in 1932, Will gave him directions for handling Congress: "Kid Congress and the Senate, don't scold them. They are just Children thats never grown up. They don't like to be corrected in Company. Don't send messages to them, send candy."[13] Roosevelt had a Democratic Congress, which permitted him sweeping executive powers; and the humorist generally approved of his methods: "That Roosevelt handled that Congress this morning just like a mother would a fretting baby. Just when any other mother would have told it to hush and be a goody baby, he didn't tell em a single thing to do. Just slipped em a piece of candy. And he left em feeling that mother had confidence in them. And they were all just tickled to death, rolling on the floor with their toes in their mouths. And goo-gooing at each other."[14]

His approval of the Roosevelt technique in handling Congress may seem somewhat contrary to his former dislike of "party line" voting; but, since the economic disease called for strong medicine, Rogers, and perhaps a majority of Americans, was ready to try anything. Thus when Roosevelt declared the Bank Holiday in March, 1932, Will wrote: "America hasn't been as happy in three years as they are today, no money, no banks, no work, no nothing, but they know they got a man in there who is wise to Congress, wise to our so-called big men. The whole country is with him, just so he does something. If he burned down the capitol we would cheer and say 'well we at least got a fire started anyhow.' We have had years of 'Don't rock the boat,' go on and sink if you want to, we just as well be swimming as like we are."[15]

Will usually said of Congress and Congressmen whatever was on his mind with a fine disregard for the consequences, but few of the targets of his wit seemed to be offended. On one occasion, when an unidentified Congressman objected to the insertion of some of Will's humor into the Congressional Record, Will replied almost at once:

When a Gentleman quoted me on the floor of Congress the other day, another member took exception and said he objected to the remarks of a Professional Joke Maker going into the Congressional Record.

Now can you beat that for jealousy among people in the same line? Calling me a Professional Joke Maker! He is right about everything but the Professional. THEY are the Professional Joke Makers. Read some of the Bills that they have passed, if you think up half the amount of funny things they can think of in one session of Congress. Besides my jokes don't do anybody any harm. You don't have to pay attention to them. But everyone of the jokes those Birds make is a LAW and hurts somebody (generally everybody). . . . And by the way, I have engaged counsel and if they ever put any more of my material in that "Record of Inefficiency" I will start suit for defamation of character. I don't want my stuff buried away where Nobody ever reads it. I am not going to lower myself enough to associate with them in a Literary way.[16]

Yet Congressmen themselves, despite the fact that they were frequent targets for his humor, were among his great admirers. In 1933, when Will announced that he was going to give up his radio program, the entire Senate sent him a telegram asking him to stay on the air and expressing enjoyment of his program. Rogers, who was pleased, wrote: "Well do you know it was one of the most pleasant things that ever happened to me. Here was the U.S. Senate that I am always kidding about, and here they come and do a nice thing like that. Why I never will get through thanking them, the mess of em. Why that petition will remain one of my most prized possessions, and the next fellow that knocks the Senate will have to answer to me. Thats my privalege and nobody elses."[17]

Will is quite exact when he speaks of "kidding" the Senate, for much of what he wrote would probably have been immediately resented had he not tempered even his most caustic criticism with disarming humor. He seemed to recognize that Americans will tolerate an attack upon their most sacred institutions if the attack is made in the spirit of fun. Although Rogers was in earnest and sincere in most of his criticism, the humorous tone and lack of malice in his writing made his remarks palatable to the public, so that even those who felt the sting of his wit seem to have harbored no grudge against him. As J.T. Winterich, a critic for the *Saturday Review of Literature,* has written, "If Will Rogers were alive today, and said some of those things without smiling, some unsmiling committee would have him under the Capitol Hill kleig lights as quick as you could say, subpoena."[18]

II   *The Depression and The New Deal*

During the postwar decade, the American economy expanded in every direction almost without interruption. Up to 1927, the advance was normal since business was expanding and profits were increasing, but soon thereafter an unnatural and unhealthy trend developed. Although business activity leveled off and commodity prices tended to decline, the price of common stocks continued to soar. The continued prosperity enjoyed under the Harding-Coolidge administrations had blinded the American people to the facts of economic law. The 1920's was a period of unbounded optimism and buoyant faith in all things American.

This America Will Rogers affectionately referred to as "Cuckooland," for he loved every square foot of it. But he suspected that the prosperity was not and could not be permanent. During the halcyon days of the Coolidge administration, he wrote, "There is no country in the history of the world that ever lived in the high class manner we do. Radio, Bath Tubs, almost Antique furniture, Pianos, Rugs — Course other Countries could have had all these things but they can't buy 'em on credit. This country is not prosperous. Its just got good credit. We live better and owe more than anybody in the world."[19] Rogers was uneasy about the American attitude toward prosperity. People were making money and buying products without having to work. It was contrary to all common sense. In Oklahoma, a man had had to work for his money, and he had paid hard cash for goods received. The allurement of installment buying seemed to Will to be basically wrong unless credit could be adequately secured.

From time to time Will cast out warnings in his column. Speculation in stocks and bonds was particularly dangerous because it was carried largely on credit; and, as he noted, credit was over-extended everywhere. But credit was hard to resist because it was offered to almost everyone, and ubiquitous salesmen were forever urging their customers to buy now and pay later in easy installments. Since this psychology appealed to the average American, most families were making payments simultaneously on a house, furniture, piano, washing machine, and vacuum cleaner. In 1927, he wrote:

You know, Cal, you been President at a mighty fortunate time in our lives. The Lord has sure been good to us. Now what are we doing to warrant that good luck any more than any other Nation? Now just how long is that going to last? Now the way we are acting, the Lord is liable to turn on us any minute; and even if He don't our good fortune can't possibly last any longer than our Natural resources. So as I look at Mexico, which hasent even been scratched as far as its natural wealth is concerned, I believe they are better off than us in the long run. It just ain't in the book for us to have the best of everything all the time. A lot of these other Nations are mighty poor, and things kinder equal up in the long run. If you got more money, the other fellow mebbe has better health; and if another's got something, why, some other will have something else. But we got too big an overbalance of everything and we better kinder start looking ahead and sorter taking stock and seeing where we are headed for. You know, I think we put too much emphasis and importance and advertising on our so-called High standard of living. I think that 'high' is the only word in that phrase that is really correct. We sure are a-living High.[20]

The highly inflated stock market was another institution of the 1920's that Rogers viewed with suspicion. There was an increasing proportion of stock held on margin — that is, not owned outright but purchased through a loan from a broker who held the stock as security. This technique fascinated many Americans who found that they could buy a great deal of stock with a small investment and pay for it from the profit realized by the rise. Few people thought of the consequences if the price of the stock went down, and few economists considered the possibility.

Will stayed out of the stock market himself. Since he worked hard for his money, he disliked taking speculative chances with it. He retained a small-town suspicion toward brokers and investment bankers whose business activities were confined to manipulating symbols of wealth rather than with products of the market. The stock market was an enigma to him: "New York can't sleep tonight wondering what the stock market will open at tomorrow. Radio has had its usual amount of static over the week-end, Steel turned out no products or received any new orders during Sunday. Montgomery Ward peddled nothing since Saturday, yet they will all change prices tomorrow. Why does this have to happen? They say it is for the good of the country. Now you tell one."[21] Why did stock go up or down, he asked? People explained it to him, but the operation did not make sense. He could never understand what the price of stock had to do with company's manufacturing and selling products.

Meanwhile, the bull market reached toward its peak in the summer of 1929. Earlier the Federal Reserve Board tried to brake the boom by increasing rediscount rates for member banks of the Reserve system. Although the immediate result was a brief drop in stock prices, the market soon recovered. Again the Federal Reserve Board tried to tighten credit by raising interest rates from five to six percent, and again an overnight dip occurred in stock prices, but the market soon recovered. The resilience of the market in the face of the Federal Reserve Board's action caused concern on Wall Street and among some bankers, but the optimism of the general public remained unchecked. Observing this fact, Will remarked, "Any business that can't survive a 1 percent raise must be skating on mighty thin ice."[22] Conservative bankers agreed, but these were in a minority; and their warning was unheeded.

On October 23, the stock market crashed. When stocks dropped an average of ten points, panic developed. There were 12,000,000 transactions on the stock exchange, and prices began plunging downward. The blackest day, however, was October 29, when an all-time record of 16,410,000 transactions took place, and the average prices of fifty leading stocks dropped nearly forty points. Since many stockholders operating on a margin were unable to raise money to save their accounts, many were sold out; and thousands of Americans saw their life savings disappear overnight. The great bull market had ended.

Will watched the panic with interest. Because he owned no stock himself, he lost no money. But many of his friends were in the market, and he commiserated with them over their losses. However, there was as yet no realization of the seriousness of the economic situation. Newspapers and commercial houses still spoke of the "sound condition" of the country. It was explained that much of the loss was on paper and did not represent real loss in the economic sense. Rogers could joke about the crash in late October: "Sure must be a great consolation to the poor people who lost their stock in the late crash to know that it has falled into the hands of Mr. Rockerfeller, who will take care of it and see that it has a good home, and never allow it to run around unprotected again."[23]

But as the initial shock wore off in November, a multitude of ills which had hitherto passed unnoticed because of the apparent prosperity of the nation began to be felt. All through the United States there was overproduction of capital goods, overambitious expansion of business concerns, and overproduction of commodities under the stimulus of installment buying. Nor was that all: the shattering of the big bull market had a profound psychological effect on the complacent American mind. No matter what the bankers and financiers might say, a major depression was underway.

Will, like most of his countrymen, did not realize the implications of the crash. His first impulse was to accept it as a good lesson for bankers and speculators who had master-minded the "gambling houses" on Wall Street: "Oh it was great while it lasted. All you had to do was buy and wait till the next morning and just pick up the paper and see how much you made — in print. But all that has changed, and I think it will be good for everything else, for after all everybody cant just live on gambling. Somebody has to do the work."[24] He felt that most of the loss had been suffered by brokers and investment houses, and he hoped that the American people might profit by the example. Because the plight of the farmer and the small businessman had not attracted his attention, Rogers did not seem to realize the severity of the situation.

Meanwhile, industrial production declined steadily; and commodity prices plunged to shocking depths. Unemployment increased daily, and by the end of 1930 stood at six million. The big depression was here. But what had caused it? Everybody had caused it, said Will: "We spent six years of wild buying and spending on credit (everything under the sun whether we needed it or not) and now we are having to pay for 'em under Mr. Hoover, and we are howling like a pet coon. P. S. This would be a great world to dance in if we didn't have to pay the fiddler."[25]

The Hoover administration tried to battle back: emergency legislation was introduced in Congress, and the nation's financial leaders offered varied remedies. "Prosperity is just around the corner" became the theme as America began to adjust to a depression economy. The American public had spent six years of wild buying on credit; now there was no money to pay the balance. The unlimited credit idea, the "buy now-pay later" theme, had backfired. "First payments," reminded the humorist, "made us think we were prosperous, and the other nineteen showed us that we were broke."[26]

A prolonged drought added to the farmer's woes during the winter of 1930-31. Will toured the Southwest for the American Red Cross, giving benefit appearances to raise money for relief. When he became concerned over the plight of the people living in the stricken area, he felt that the Federal government owed a responsibility to the people who were hungry. Granaries and warehouses were overflowing with wheat purchased by the government in a futile effort to support farm prices. After the tour, Will wrote in 1931: "If you live under a Government and it dont provide some means of you getting work when you really want it and will do it, why then there is something wrong. You cant just let the people starve, so if you dont give em work, and you dont give em food, or money to buy it, why what are they to do? What is the matter with our Country anyhow? With all our brains in high positions, and all our boasted organizations, thousands of our folks are starving, or on the verge of it. Millions of bushels of wheat are in the Granaries at the lowest price in twenty years. Why cant there be some means of at least giving everybody all the bread they wanted anyhow?"[27]

Will did not advocate a "dole" for the farmer, for he firmly believed that the American people did not want to be given a "free handout." What the people wanted was a chance to work and earn a living. In a radio broadcast, he said sarcastically:

We used to be told that depression was just a state of mind, but starvation has changed that impression, depression is a state of health, its moved from the mind to the stomach, and it ain't really depression either, its just a return to normalcy, we are just getting back to earth and it dont look natural to us anymore, we are back to two-bit meals and cotton underwear, and off the $1.50 steaks and silk under rompers. The trouble with us is America is just muscle bound from holding a steering wheel, the only place we are callused from work is the bottom of our driving toe.[28]

Despite the efforts of the Hoover administration to solve the nation's problem, economic conditions grew steadily worse. Unemployment figures mounted daily; by the end of 1931 over eleven million people were unemployed. Panhandlers lined the streets, shanty towns sprang up around industrial areas, and long bread lines formed outside private and local relief headquarters. Prices for all goods and commodities dropped sharply; factories curtailed production or closed their doors; employers cut wages; and more and more people were without work. Nothing that the Hoover administration attempted gave more than temporary relief. As the election year approached, it was obvious that not only the President but bankers and businessmen had suffered a loss of prestige. The results of the 1932 election were decisive; Franklin D. Roosevelt won an overwhelming victory, and the Democrats won control of Congress.

After the election, Will wrote a public letter to both Hoover and Roosevelt. He told Hoover that there was nothing personal in the vote against him, that the people were simply looking for a change. He gave Roosevelt some simple advice: do something. The country did not have to wait long for action. Rogers was delighted when Roosevelt, on the day of his inauguration, called Congress into emergency session and proclaimed a national bank holiday. He wrote: "The first move was to close the banks. He beat the depositors by about 24 hours. They would have closed em anyhow. But here is the difference, when a depositor closes one it stays closed, but when the President closed one, it has a relapse and opens later. That was the one big thing that he did that really started the whole 'Back to Normalcy.' . . . The Republican thinks the boat shouldent be rocked. The Democrat says, 'Rocked bedambded, why sit here and starve in it? Go ahead and turn it over, maby the bottom side has got some barnacles on it we can eat.' It dident take Mr. Roosevelt long to see that a major operation was necessary. Asparin wouldent do a thing for the patient but prolong the agony. He had had that for years."[29] This study of Will Rogers is not the place to review the achievements of the Roosevelt administration, but never before in American history had so much important legislation been passed in so short a time as during the special session of the Seventy-third Congress.

Will approved of virtually all of the New Deal which was concerned with domestic problems. He was enthusiastic about the National Recovery Act, which he felt was an aid to the small businessman; he applauded the Agricultural Adjustment Act for its consideration of the farmer; and he believed that the Public Works Adminis-

tration would relieve unemployment. At the request of the administration, the humorist toured the country in 1933 extolling the virtues
of the National Recovery Act, which he explained as a code of fair
ethics for businessmen. He called it, "decency by government control."[30] He even backed Roosevelt's plan of controlling inflation by
calling in all gold to the government reserve and by standardizing the
price at thirty-five dollars an ounce, which had the effect of devaluat-
ing the dollar to 59.6 cents. After a visit to the Capitol, he wrote, "I
tell you folks, I came away from Washington last week with the idea
that the little fellow has got somebody in his corner in Washington.
I don't mean the Administration is against big business. There are
hundreds and thousands of big ones entering into this thing with
enthusiasm, and with their money and their whole hearts; but for
the first time in years the big man comes to Washington the same as
the little man. If this administration ever goes under, it should have
written on it's tombstone: 'Perished through trying to give the little
fellow a square deal.' "[31]

But, as the time went on, Will became somewhat critical of some
aspects of the New Deal program. He distrusted some of the
President's advisors, the so-called "brain trust," which included such
college professors as Raymond Moley and Rexford A. Tugwell.
These were smart men, he admitted, but they tended to be theorists
and idealists. "A professor gets all his knowledge out of a book, but a
politician, as bad as he is, does have an understanding of human
nature and the mob."[32] When the National Recovery Act was
declared unconstitutional by the Supreme Court, he attributed its
failure to its complicated structure. There were too many codes, and
too many private interest groups who wanted to be exempt from the
code. Human nature, the humorist concluded, had not changed.
Businessmen spent time and money trying to evade the law. In fact,
said Will, business found an answer to the New Deal; it hired smarter
lawyers than Roosevelt's "brain trusters" to find legal methods of
evading restriction.[33]

The New Deal, of course, was and is still a controversial issue. It
engendered a new philosophy of government for the United States,
which has been variously praised or condemned according to the
effect it had on the individual. By and large, Will thought it effective
in combating the obvious ills of the Depression, but he appeared to be
doubtful about the permanent effect of some of the liberal social
theories. Just forty-five days before his final trip with Wiley Post, he

reviewed the achievements of the Roosevelt administration. It had been exciting and effective, he admitted; so much so that he ended his column, "a fellow can't afford to die now with all this excitement going on."[34]

III *Soldiers' Bonus*

At the close of World War I, the abrupt demobilization of soldiers, combined with the dismissal of war workers from industry, caused a serious unemployment problem. The veterans were championed by the newly formed American Legion, which petitioned Congress for legislation to benefit the servicemen and demands for some kind of bonus began to circulate by 1920 in Congress. Action, however, was not forthcoming; for Congress was committed to a tax-reduction program following the war.

Will Rogers was heartily in favor of a soldiers' bonus. He himself had not been required to serve in the army because of his age, thirty-seven years, and because of his three children. Yet during the war years, he had given unstintingly of his time to Liberty Bond rallies and played innumerable soldier shows. He felt his responsibilities deeply and pledged to pay one hundred dollars a week to the Salvation Army and American Red Cross during the war period. Moreover, Will felt strongly about the war profiteers who had stayed at home and reaped the benefits of war economy, while the soldiers, who were denied a bonus, had worked in the army for twenty-one dollars a month. He suggested that in the next war, capital as well as manpower be drafted:

You will hear the question, "Yes, but how could you do it?" Say, you take a Boy's life, don't you? When you take Boys away you take everything they have in the World, that is, their life. You send them to war and part of that life you don't lose you let him come back with it. Perhaps you may use all of it. Well, that's the way to do with wealth. Take all he has, give him a bare living the same as you do the Soldier. Give him the same allowance as the Soldier — all of us that stay home. The Government should own everything we have, use what it needs to conduct the whole expenses of the war and give back what is left. if there is any, the same as you give back to the Boy what he has left. There can be no Profiteering. The Government owns everything till the war is over. Every Man, Woman and Child, from Henry Ford and John D. down, get their Dollar and a Quarter a day the same as the Soldier. The only way a man could profiteer in war like that would be raise more Children. But, no, it will never get anywhere. The rich will say it ain't practical, and the poor will never get a chance to find out if it is or not.[35]

The soldiers' bonus was a delicate issue in Congress, for it feared alienating the large number of voters who had served in the armed forces. But, when a bonus bill was finally passed by the legislature in 1923, President Warren Harding promptly vetoed it. Rogers, indignant at the action of the administration, felt that the veterans deserved some compensation for the time lost from their civilian occupations while serving in the army. When the President vetoed the bill and the Senate upheld the veto, he wrote: "My opinion of the bonus is based on what I heard uttered to the Soldiers in the days when we needed them, when they were looked on as not a Political Organization with a few hundred votes to cast, but as the pick of One Hundred Million people, the Saviours of Civilization. You promised them everything but the kitchen stove if they would go to war. We promised them EVERYTHING, and all they got was $1.25 a day and some knitted sweaters and sox."[36]

Rogers recalled that the men who had stayed at home and had worked in the war industries not only got high wages, but also time and a half for overtime work. These promises made to the soldiers during wartime, he believed, were debts of gratitude which should be paid. "Now if a man is against it, why dont he at least come out and tell the real truth. 'I dont want to spare the money to pay the Boys.' I think the best insurance in the World against another War is to take care of the Boys who fought in the last one. YOU MAY WANT TO USE THEM AGAIN."[37] A bonus bill was finally passed in 1924, over President Calvin Coolidge's veto, but it was restrictive. The payments of the bonus were not made in cash, but in a twenty-year, paid-up endowment policy which carried an interest rate of 4 percent and which could not be cashed until 1944. Thus the bonus was of little value to the veteran at the time.

IV *The Scopes Evolution Trial*

Among the dangerous ideas which certain conservative Americans hoped to suppress in the postwar years were those which challenged the old standards of religious orthodoxy. These fundamentalists sought to purge all churches of any type of religious modernism. Although Rogers had been reared in the Methodist church, he had developed a tolerance for all religious faiths. "Whatever way you serve your God," he said, "will never get one word of argument or condemnation out of me."[38] Consequently, the militant spirit of the fundamentalists, exemplified in the crusading of Billy Sunday and in other older evangelistic preachers, was abhorrent to him.

However, the fundamentalists made progress in the South; and several southern states, including Tennessee, passed laws forbidding the teaching of Charles Darwin's theory of evolution in public schools. When the American Civil Liberties Union quickly announced that it would back any school teacher who would test the law in court, a young biology teacher in Dayton, Tennessee, agreed to cooperate. John Thomas Scopes lectured to his class on the Darwinian evolutionary theory, and he was arrested for teaching this departure from the biblical version of creation and was brought to trial in July, 1925. But Scopes was almost forgotten during the trial because of the legal talent involved: William Jennings Bryan joined the prosecution, and the defense was placed in the hands of Clarence Darrow, one of the ablest criminal lawyers in America.

Will read of the controversy with some interest. He had never favored the fundamentalist position, although he had never openly espoused the evolutionary theory. Just before the trial, however, he openly stated his position on religious tolerance: "The Lord put all these millions of people over the earth. They don't all agree how they got here and ninety percent dont care. But he was pretty wise when he did see to it that they agree on one thing (whether Christian, Heathen, or Mohammedan) and that is the better life you live the better you will finish."[39]

Rogers did not attend the trial in Dayton, but he read the newspaper accounts of its progress. The atmosphere was not one of religious piety despite the religious revivalists who converged to preach to curious crowds about the fate of religion. There was a carnival air in the streets where lemonade venders and hot-dog caterers peddled their wares. Because of the heat, the judge, defendant, and counsel stripped to their shirt sleeves in court. Will the humorist particularly viewed Bryan's participation with a good deal of skepticism: "Andrew Jackson brought undying fame to the glorious state of Tennessee. . . . But it remained for the product of the corn tassels of Nebraska and the underwater realtor from Florida to bring a dignified commonwealth onto the comic pages of every periodical in the world. 'Hickory' Jackson's work of a lifetime has been all undone by the self-advertisement of William Jennings Bryan. . . . Tennessee claims they didn't descent from a monkey, but their actions in this case prove otherwise. . . . No man should have to prove in court what he is, or what he comes from."[40]

Will, who felt that Bryan was using the trial as a political opportunity to gain personal publicity, wrote: "Bryan should appear for nothing. He ought to pay Scopes fine. It has been almost like a Democrat convention for Bryan. It is the most publicity any politician ever had in an off-election year. You can't stop a man from thinking, neither do I think Bryan could start a serious man thinking. These fellows who honestly believe that their great great grandfather was as proficient with his toes as with his fingers, they have just as much right to seriously believe that as he has to believe he is the second Messiah and that Nebraska is the modern Manger."[41] The Democrat party was still looking for a leader, and Will apparently believed that Bryan was making political capital of the situation with that ambition in mind.

Although Rogers himself did not know a great deal about Darwin and the theory of evolution, he did recognize the importance of free discussion about it. Moreover, he had discussed the trial with prominent men whose opinions he respected, and he shared their view that narrow religious prejudice leads to distrust and hatred. He wrote: "I don't know how I got here but I will just stay and take my chance at the end, rather than Bryan's chance if he willfully stirs up religious hatred among his fellow men."[42]

The most dramatic moment of the trial came when the defense summoned Bryan to the stand to testify as an expert on the Bible. Under Darrow's questioning, the fundamentalist leader proclaimed his belief that the whale swallowed Jonah, that Joshua made the sun stand still, and that the world was created in 4004 B.C. When Bryan took the stand, Will began to find humor in the situation. Already the newspapers had had a field day at the expense of the Great Commoner, but Bryan never gave up. Toward the end of the trial, when he made a final impassioned plea, basing his oration on man's intellectual superiority over the monkey, Rogers made the following comment: "If I was in either one of these men's places, I wouldn't spend the best years of my Chautauqua life trying to prove or disprove my ancestry. With conditions the Democrat party is in at the present, instead of trying to prove he didn't descend from a monkey, Bryan had better be trying to prove he didn't descend from a Democrat."[43]

As Will pointed out, the Scopes trial proved nothing. The only question at issue in the trial was whether Scopes had taught evolution. As this was admitted, the result was a foregone conclusion. Theoretically, the fundamentalists won, for the law was upheld; in reality they lost, for civilized opinion everywhere regarded the trial with amusement, and the slow drift toward modernism continued.

V *National Party Conventions*

Of all the national events which Will Rogers covered as a columnist, he loved best to attend the Presidential nominating conventions. Although he was aware that the conventions were usually controlled and expertly directed by the professional party leaders and that the delegates to the convention had little to say about the selection of the party's candidate, he also recognized that the color and excitement of the conventions exhibited all of the flamboyant aspects of the American political scene. He wrote biting and satiric comments about the activities at the conventions, but he never tired of the keynote addresses, the nominating speeches, the readings of the party platforms, the polling of the delegations — all of the proceedings through which the final selections of presidential candidates were made.

The first convention which Will attended was the Republican convention of 1924 held in Cleveland. The convention was a dull and uninteresting affair largely because the nomination of President Calvin Coolidge was a foregone conclusion. With no noticeable political problems confronting him during the postwar boom of the 1920's, Coolidge had no serious challenger in the party. In fact, as Will wrote, "Coolidge could have been nominated by post card. Those misled delegates will have just as much chance to really nominate him as a Bow Legged girl would have at our Stage Door."⁴⁴ Will's prediction was accurate. Coolidge was nominated on the first roll call, and Charles Dawes was later selected as his running mate.

From Cleveland, Will traveled to New York to watch what he called the Democrat "Follies." He was not disappointed. The Democratic National Convention of 1924 set records for longevity and partisanship. The party was widely split on almost every issue: the "wets" versus the "drys," the East and North versus the South and West, and Al Smith versus William McAdoo. After listening to the nominating speeches which consumed the better part of a day, Will wrote, "Talk about Presidential Timber, why, Man they had whole Lumber yards of it here. There was so many being nominated that some of the men making the nominating Speeches had never even met the men they were nominating. I know they had not from the way they talked about them. A guy from Utah talked so long and loud that all of us couldent see how it could be anybody in the world he was nominating but Brigham Young — that matchless father — but he crossed everybody by seconding McAdoo's nomination."[45]

The convention seemed endless as the party leaders attempted to frame a party platform suitable for the party and acceptable to the widely divergent partisan groups. When the platform was finally presented, Will wrote,

Well, it was 6:30 and they had just read the platform. I had it before me, forty-five pages. If it had come out in the open on every question and told just where they stood, they could have saved themselves, not only forty-two pages of paper, but perhaps the election in November. When you straddle a thing it takes a long time to explain it. It favors fixing everything the Republicans have ruined, keeping everything they haven't, right up to its present standard. In the Republican platform at Cleveland they promised to do better. I dont think they have done so bad this time. Everybody's broke but them.[46]

In the polling of delegates to choose a candidate, it soon became apparent that the contest was a standoff between McAdoo and Al Smith. During one hundred ballotings, neither of these men could secure the necessary two-thirds majority. Thus, in one of those inexplicable compromises that sometimes mark political conventions, John W. Davis of New York was nominated on the 103rd ballot. Will commented sardonically on the nomination:

Who said miracles don't happen? Didn't the Democratic National Convention nominate a man at last? That should bring more people back to religion than any other one thing. It has been a demonstration of faith, because, after all God is good. This convention wound up in a personal triumph for William Jennings Bryan. . . . But Mr. Bryan even improves on a bear; a bear hibernates all Winter, but Bryan hibernates for four years and then emerges, and has a celebration every four years at every Democratic Convention. . . . No one has ever been able to understand the unique and uncanny power he seems to hold over the Democratic party, especially near nominating time. . . . When he came out *against* Davis, Davis was a nominated man. Those eleven hundred delegates said, "If Bryan is so set against him he must be the right man."[47]

As Will had predicted, President Calvin Coolidge had little difficulty in his bid for reelection. The country was prosperous; even the farmers had little to complain about. As the humorist put it, "The result was just as big a surprise as the announcement that Christmas was coming in December. The Republicans mopped up, the Democrats gummed up. . . . You can't beat an administration by attacking it. You have to show some plan on improving it."[48] At the end of Coolidge's administration in 1928, the United States was enjoying a wave of prosperity. The great bull market was in full swing; to many people, it appeared that the Republicans were responsible for it. Although Coolidge refused to run for another term, the Republicans were still confident and complacent; for, with Coolidge out of the running, the way was open for Secretary of Commerce Herbert Hoover, former director of war relief in Belgium and later Food Administrator under the Wilson administration. Hoover was not the choice of Wall Street, or the Farm Block, or even the party leaders; but his record of efficiency and integrity had won the admiration of the American people.

In 1928, when the Republican Party held its convention in Kansas City, Will arrived early to interview party leaders and speak to the delegates. Hoover was the clear choice of the delegates, he learned, and there was no strong opposition to prevent him from receiving the nomination. Will attended the opening session of the convention and listened to the keynote address by Simeon D. Fess:

A Keynote Speech is Press notices of the Republican party written by their own members. Here are just a few things that I bet you didn't know the Republicans were responsible for: Radio Telephone, Baths, Automobiles, Savings Accounts, Law Enforcement, Workmen living in houses, and a living wage for Senators. The Democrats had brought on War, pestilence, debts, Disease, Bo Weevil, Gold Teeth, need of farm relief, suspenders, floods, famine, and Tom Heflin. . . . Once I thought sure he was referring to "Our Saviour" till they told me, "no, it was Coolidge." The way he rated 'em was Coolidge, The Lord, and then Lincoln.[49]

The convention quickly went about its business. The 1928 platform was virtually a repetition of the 1924 platform. When the polling took place, Hoover was nominated on the first ballot and Senator Charles Curtis of Kansas was nominated for the vice-presidency. Will wrote: " 'Wow.' She is all over, Hoover and Curtis. The Republican party owed Curtis something, but I didn't think they would be so low down as to pay him that way. . . . Another preacher prayed this morning . . . he wanted us to 'look to the Hills for wisdom' and here we were nominating Charley Curtis from the plains of Kansas, Where a five foot ash heap would constitute a precipice."[50]

The 1928 Democratic convention, which was held in Houston, lacked the acridness and bitterness which had been present at its convention four years earlier. The urban contingent had prevailed over both southern and rural opposition, and Governor Alfred Smith of New York came to the convention virtually assured of the nomination. The only excitement was about the issue of Prohibition which, as Will predicted, both parties were afraid to face. Governor Smith personally advocated the repeal of the Eighteenth Amendment, but the Democratic platform called for enforcement of Prohibition. Will, who had a great time in Houston, had lunch with Mrs. Woodrow Wilson and visited with Jesse Jones and Bernard Baruch. At the opening session, he wrote, "It took 20 minutes of steady hammering to get order enough for them to listen to a prayer. . . . The meeting didn't last long. It was the shortest Democratic meeting on record. Some man prayed, I didn't get his name or political faith. But from his earnestness, I should say he was a Democrat. He not only asked for guidance, but he wisely hinted for VOTES."[51]

After the keynote speech and the presentation of the party platform, Franklin D. Roosevelt placed the name of Alfred Smith in nomination just as he had done four years earlier in New York. Will wrote:

Franklin Roosevelt, a fine and wonderful man who has devoted his life to nominating Al Smith did his act from memory. . . . It was a fine speech. It always has been, but it's always been ahead of its time. Now he has 'em believing it. The only part I didn't agree with is where he said that Al was "Good to Women and Children and Dumb Animals", and he insinuated that the Republican President and nominee were not. Now, Franklin, you are wrong about the Republicans and the Dumb Animals. They just thrive on Dumb Animals. They are like Lincoln with the poor. They must love them for they have so many of them in the party. And I even believe that the Republicans like children. Not perhaps as children, but they are the material of which voters are made in a few years. So I believe the Republicans would be kind to 'em just so they would grow into manhood quicker.[52]

Despite the animosity to Al Smith's stand on Prohibition and his Catholic religion, he was nominated on the first ballot; and Joseph Robinson of Arkansas was selected as the vice-presidential nominee. However, the seeds of defeat were sown at the convention, for many

Democrats who were staunch "drys" or even stauncher Protestants were determined to cross party lines during the election. Will had no illusions about the election of 1928, for the Republican platform of "Prosperity, Peace and Plenty" was irresistible. The day before the election, Will offered this evaluation of the two candidates: "Hoover says the tariff will be kept up. Smith says the tariff will not be lowered. Hoover is strongly in favor of prosperity. Smith highly indorses prosperity. Hoover wants no votes merely on account of religion. Smith wants no votes on solely religious ground. Both would accept Mohammaden votes if offered. Hoover would like to live in the White House. Smith is not adverse to living in the White House. In order to get there either one will promise the voters anything from perpetual motion to eternal salvation."[53]

But the result of the election was never in doubt. Hoover carried forty states. It was, as Will put it, "the greatest lesson in geography that New York City ever had. They never knew so many people lived west of the Hudson River."[54] But the Hoover honeymoon was of short duration. In October, 1929, came the great stock market crash which shook the economic structure of the United States. Economic reality finally caught up with the American dream, and Hoover was tagged in the three years that followed 1929 as the "depression" President and the Republicans as the "depression" party.

The year 1932 looked as bright to the Democrats as it was black for the Republicans. Both parties were holding their conventions in Chicago, with the Republicans meeting first. Will arrived early for what he termed "a convention held for no reason at all" for the Republicans had to stand with Hoover and Curtis. The toughest job at the convention, said Will, is that of the keynote speaker: "If he 'points to accomplishments' he is sunk, and if he 'views with alarm', he is sunk. So we are just liable to get two solid hours on the weather."[55] President Hoover had a firm grip on the party machinery, and he was renominated on the first ballot with Charles Curtis as his running mate.

The Democrats came to Chicago highly optimistic. Candidates were plentiful for the nomination, including Alfred Smith who wanted another chance. But Governor Franklin D. Roosevelt of New York came to the convention with a large number of delegates pledged to him in advance. Will wrote: "All you can hear is 'Will they stop Roosevelt?' Well they dident stop him from getting six or seven hundred delegates. . . . Anyhow its a good spot for a delegate to be in. Never was a deligate so much in demand."[56] Actually, it was a little late for the other candidates; for the smoothness and efficiency of Franklin Roosevelt's organization won him the nomination on the fourth ballot. John Nance Garner of Texas was selected as the vice-presidential nominee.

Will thoroughly enjoyed the convention. Not only was he introduced and asked to make a few remarks to the assembled delegates, but his home state of Oklahoma placed him in nomination and cast twenty-two votes for him as a "favorite son." Will's response was characteristic:

I was sitting there in the press stand asleep and wasent bothering a soul when they woke me up and said Oklahoma had started me on the way to the White House with 22 votes. . . . Course I realize now that I should have stayed awake and protected my interest but it was the only time I had ever entered national politics and I dident look for the boys to nick me so quick. . . . Now I dont want you to think I am belittling the importance of those 22 votes. They was worth something there at a time Roosevelt's bunch would have given me secretary of State for that 22. . . . And what do I do — go to sleep and wake up without even the support of the Virgin Islands. . . . Now what am I? Just another ex-Democratic Presidential candiate. There's thousands of 'em. Well, the whole thing has been a terrible lesson to me and nothing to do but start in and live it down.[57]

Will's attitude toward events of national importance was curiously ambivalent. Politically, he could not be classified as either a conservative or a liberal since he generally tended to take a middle-of-the-road approach on most political issues. He was not interested in affiliating with either political party, preferring to think of himself as an independent, nonpartisan observer of the political scene. But, as Norris Yates observed about Will's political detachment: "Aloofness toward factions was necessary if Will was indeed to speak for all the people, but it also stemmed from his real indifference to the outcome of party squabbles."[58] As a result of this detachment, Will seemed to regard the political scene as an entertaining spectacle which he, as an observer and interpreter, reported to the American people.

CHAPTER 4

Observer of His Age:
The International Scene

DURING the ten-year period following World War I, the United States played a prominent and varied role in the world of diplomacy. Numerous inconsistencies developed, which were to be expected in a country which had never had any well-defined, long-range, international policy. Extreme nationalism was demonstrated in the rejection of the League of Nations and in the erection of high protective walls against imports and immigration; on the other hand, the United States showed some willingness to make concessions in the matter of debts, reparations, and disarmament.

I *Foreign Relations*

Will Rogers' interest in foreign affairs had developed during World War I when he had been an enthusiastic supporter of President Wilson's foreign policy. During the postwar years, however, he had become more and more distrustful of international dealings. He viewed with suspicion the traditional methods of diplomacy, which called for high-level conferences among nations on world affairs. He wrote: "There is one thing no Nation can ever accuse us of and that is secret Diplomacy. Our Foreign dealings are an Open Book, generally a Check Book."[1] The failure of European nations to pay back war loans was a sore point with Rogers, as it apparently was with millions of Americans. He felt that the United States had been out-maneuvered in the Versailles treaty, and he doubted the wisdom of continued diplomatic conferences with European nations.

Meanwhile, the United States, although refusing to join the League of Nations, tried to promote world peace through the Washington Naval Conference in 1921-1922. The conference was aimed toward stopping an apparent armament race among the United States, Great Britain, and Japan — all of which had developed ambitious programs for increased naval construction following World War I. In November, 1921, diplomats from the three great naval powers, together with diplomatic representatives from France and Italy, met in Washington, D. C. for disarmament discussion. At the first meeting, Secretary of State Hughes bluntly proposed a ten-year holiday in the construction of capital ships and the scrapping of current capital ships toward the establishment of ratio of a 5:5:3 in tonnage among the navies of Great Britain, Japan, and the United States. The Hughes proposal met strong resistance; but, by February 6, 1922, several important decisions were reached: the United States, England, Japan, France, and Italy agreed to scrap a specified amount of naval tonnage of capital ships. In addition, the Pacific powers — the United States, Great Britain, and Japan — joined with China, Portugal, Belgium, France, Italy, and the Netherlands in subscribing to the Nine Power Pact which agreed to guarantee the sovereignty of China.

Although the achievements of the Washington Conference seemed great at the time, Will was dubious about the naval limitation agreement. Not to build more capital ships seemed sensible to him, but to destroy capital ships already built and paid for seemed unwise. The first of the capital ships to be scrapped by the United States was the *Washington,* which was towed out to sea on December 1, 1923, and destroyed by gun fire. Rogers wrote:

Well, we were all last week trying to sink our greatest Battleship, the Washington. Here is a Boat we had spent 35 millions on, and we go out and sink it. And the funny part is that it cost us more to sink it than it did to build it. We shot all the ammunition we had left over from the war into it and those big Guns on the Texas they were using, they only are good for so many shots during their lifetime. So we spoiled the Guns of our next best boat trying to sink the best one. A great many people don't understand just how this sinking come about. You see we had a conference over here a few years ago. It was called by America. We were building a lot of Battleships and we had plenty of money to do it on, and it looked like in a couple of years we might have the largest Navy in the World. Well, the League of Nations gathering in Paris had attracted a lot of attention and got quite a lot of publicity, none of which had been shared in this country by the Democrats. So, when the Republicans got in, they conceived the idea of a publicity stunt for the Republicans. Why not then have a conference? But what would they confer about? The League of Nations had conferred about six months, and in that time had taken up about every question on the Calendar. So Secretary Hughes happened to think of an idea: "Let us confer on sinking Battleships." Well, the idea was so original that they immediately made him the Toastmaster. You see, up to then, Battleships had always been sunk by the enemy, and when he proposed to sink them yourself it was the most original thought that had ever percolated the mind of a Statesman. So, when we communicated the idea to England and Japan that we had an idea whereby we would sink some of our own Battleships, why they come over so fast, even the Butler wasn't dressed to receive them when they arrived. England was willing to tear her blueprints on planned building into half, Japan was willing to give up her dreams of having more ships on the seas than any nation and stop building up to 3/5 of the size of England and America, and Secretary Hughes met that with, "Now, Gentlemen, I will show you what America is prepared to do. FOR EVERY BATTLESHIP YOU FELLOWS DON'T BUILD AMERICA WILL SINK ONE." Now they are talking of having another Naval Disarmament Conference. We can only stand one more. If they ever have a second one we will have to borrow a Boat to go to it. You see, we don't like to ever have the start on any Nation in case of war. We figure it looks better to start late and come from behind. If we had a big Navy some Nation would just be kicking on us all the time. Sinking your own Boats is a military strategy that will always remain in the sole possession of America.[2]

Will, who had been an advocate of a large and powerful American Navy since the Theodore Roosevelt administration, believed that England's supremacy on the sea was the reason for that nation's strong diplomatic position in world affairs. If the United States wished to emulate British success in diplomacy, a large navy and a powerful army were essential.

The second part of the Washington Conference, the Nine Power Agreement to respect the sovereignty of China, seems to have suited Will. He apparently felt that imperialism violated the basic traditional philosophy of the natural right of all peoples to self-determination; consequently, nothing was more calculated to arouse his ire than a large nation's moving into the territory of a small or less powerful nation on the pretext of "protecting its interests." When the United States protested to Mexico about the possible seizure of American-owned oil property in Mexico, Rogers wrote:

America has a great habit of always talking about protecting American interests in some foreign Country. PROTECT 'EM HERE AT HOME! There is more American Interests right here than anywhere. If an American goes to Mexico and his Horse dies, we send them a Note wanting American Interests preserved and the horse paid for. If America is not good enough for you to live in and make money in, why, then you are privileged to go to some other Country. But don't ask protection from a Country that was not good enough for you. If you want to make money out of a Country, why, take out their

Citizenship Papers and join them. Don't use one Country for Money and another for convenience. The difference in our exchange of people with Mexico is; they send workmen here to work, while we send Americans there to "work" Mexico. America and England, especially, are regular old Busybodies when it comes to telling somebody else what to do. But you notice they (England and America) never tell each other what to do. You bet your life they don't! Big Nations are always talking about Honor. Yet England promised to protect France against Germany, IF FRANCE WOULD PAY THEM WHAT THEY OWED THEM. They act as a Police Force for pay. What is the consequence? As soon as Germany gets strong enough so she thinks she can lick both of them there will be another War.[3]

Will applauded the Petroleum Law passed by the Mexican government. From his viewpoint, the exploitation of natural resources of another country was robbery. When Secretary of State Kellogg sent a diplomatic note to Mexico on behalf of the involved oil companies, Rogers was irritated. He commented ironically that the United States was very careful in its diplomatic dealings with any nation with a powerful navy, but it was very demanding where the rights of a small nation were concerned. "Trace any war," he wrote, "and you will find some Nation trying to tell some other Nation how to run their business."[4]

It seemed especially ironical to the humorist that the great nations of the world should be so concerned with China. During the Civil War in China in 1925, he noted with sarcasm that every nation seemed to regard its own sovereignty as being threatened. The "open door" policy, he noted, opened only one way. "What a wail would go up," he wrote, "if China decided she needed a Coaling Station or Naval Base to protect her interests in Liverpool."[5] When England sent a fleet of warships to Hong Kong to protect British lives and property, Rogers wrote: "Of course, the British were there protecting their interests with a fleet as is usual in any private argument held anywhere in the world. . . . They are trying to get a gunboat to Dayton, Tennessee, to see that British ancestral tails are not trampled on."[6] And, when the United States sent Marines to Nicaragua, Will commented, "Even America is stealing their stuff. You can't pick up a paper without seeing where the Marines were landed to keep some Nation from shooting each other, and if necessary, we shoot them to keep them from shooting each other."[7] Mexico, China, and Nicaragua, so Will reasoned, had an inherent right to make their own laws and govern their own affairs. Unwarranted intervention by the United States, or any European country, was unjustifiable.

Meanwhile, despite the Washington Conference, the signatory powers, except the United States, continued building the destroyers, the cruisers, and the submarines that were not limited by the treaty. Because the United States seemed complacent in affairs of armament, even failing to maintain its allotted quota of capital ships, Rogers was shocked at the attitude of the administration and the people because it reflected unconcern about national defense. He believed, in general, that a strong army and navy were essential for the preservation of peace; in particular, he felt that the security of the United States was jeopardized by the American attitude toward the Japanese as expressed by the Japanese Exclusion Act of 1923 and by the disregard of Japanese naval strength in the Pacific. When the American fleet was holding battle maneuvers in the Pacific, he wrote: "This trip was planned with our Pacific fleet to impress Japan with the size of it. That was not necessary. Japan knows more about our war strength now than either of our Secretaries of War or Navy."[8]

If Will had a natural distrust of peace conferences, his suspicions were confirmed by the Kellogg-Briand Pact, signed in Paris on August 27, 1928, by fifteen nations. These nations solemnly declared that they condemned war as an instrument of national policy, and they affirmed that all future disputes or conflicts would be settled by peaceful means. Public support of the Kellogg-Briand Pact in America was overwhelming, and the Senate ratified it by a vote of 85-1. Rogers differed from the majority opinion on the pact. He had spent the summer of 1926 in Europe and had visited with prominent men in England, France, Italy, and Spain. What they told him and what he had observed in Europe made him pessimistic about the prospects for permanent peace. Despite the general economic prosperity of Western Europe, there were still petty jealousies and national rivalries. The old wounds of war still smarted in Germany, France, England, and Italy. Germany owed reparations to France and England and could not pay its debt. England and France owed the United States and wanted a debt settlement. The United States, Will discovered, was neither popular nor trusted anywhere in Europe.

These things caused him to doubt the efficacy of any mutual pact for peace. He wrote: "Just when Secretary Kellogg had his 'no more war' plan all going good and about ready to sign up, why England, Japan, and France came through with the old diplomatic clause which says, 'we agree in principal but.' Well there was the but. 'We are heartily against all wars, unless, of course, we should see fit to do a little fighting ourselves. Then, of course, this agreement would be null and void. But we certainly join you in preventing others from having the pleasure of fighting."[9]

Will's cynicism about the Kellogg-Briand Pact was based on his observations of the attitude of European nations toward disarmament. During his tour of Europe, he found that national rivalry was so intense that disarmament was considered tantamount to national suicide. A disarmament conference, or a peace pact, cannot work, he said, when in Europe, "France and England think just as much of each other as two rival Gangs of Chicago bootleggers. . . . A Frenchman and an Italian love each other just about like Minneapolis and St. Paul. Spain and France have the same regard for each other as Ft. Worth and Dallas. . . . Russia hates everybody so bad it would take her a week to pick out the one she hates the most. Poland is ararin' to Fight somebody so bad that they just haul off and Punch themselves in the jaw to keep in practice."[10]

Moreover, for Americans who might not understand the fear which existed between European nations, he explained: "Just suppose you let France change places with Canada, and Germany change places with Mexico, and England with Cuba and Japan with Hawaii — then you'd see if we in the United States would be over-anxious to Disarm. Say Boss, if I didn't have any more friends than some of these Nations have around them, I not only would not disarm but I wouldn't go to bed — I would stay up and watch all night."[11]

In 1930, Rogers attended the London Conference, sponsored by Great Britain, which opened on January 21 to discuss the problem of naval limitation of small ships not covered by the Washington agreement. When he arrived in London on January 17, Will took one look at the situation, talked to some of the delegates, and wired home the following day: "The American delegation arrived this afternoon. . . . They brought eighteen young typewriters with 'em. That's four and a half blonds to the delegate. And I can write in long hand, left-handed, every thing that will be done here next month."[12] As the conference developed, and closed sessions were announced, he began to feel that the United States would be outmaneuvered by England and Japan. "There is some tough babies over here," Will warned. "Talk about taking boats away from them. There is a delegation here that wouldn't give up a rowboat to see eternal salvation."[13]

After Will had spent ten days at the conference, he returned home without much hope of any enduring results. National security was the theme of every nation involved, and there seemed little chance of avoiding an armament race. On his return, Rogers remarked that he could write on the head of a pin all that had been accomplished at the conference and still have room for an additional message. Later he wrote:

Well, the whole thing was nothing but a Democratic convention, with a silk hat on. The king made the best speech and then showed his real intelligence by leaving. When speaking he was facing the American delegation. When he went out he happened to think, so he sent four men back and they carried the gold throne chair out. That will go on record as the first lack of confidence shown. We stood during one speech, sat through eight and slept through twelve; three solid hours of compliments and not a single rowboat sunk. When Mr. Stimson said we will stay here till the world disarms, his wife says, "My lord!" and the rest of the wives shook hands with me and bid me farewell forever.[14]

However, the conference on naval ratios met with a mixed reaction from Americans. Although, generally, the liberals hailed it as a step toward the permanent stabilization of armament and toward world peace, the isolationists thought the treaty too restrictive and detrimental to the interests of the United States. Nevertheless, the agreement of the three major naval powers to attempt limitation seemed encouraging at the time.

II *The Manchurian Dispute*

Meanwhile, the Kellogg-Briand Pact received a severe test. In September, 1931, Japan began open warfare with China in Manchuria, moving Japanese troops onto the mainland to protect "Japan's sovereignty" in the area. An unexplained explosion on the Japanese-controlled South Manchurian railway near Mukden was the pretext which Japan used to justify the invasion of Manchuria. The League of Nations invoked the Kellogg-Briand Pact to no purpose, and the proposed economic sanctions to enforce treaty obligations were rejected by the western powers. Hence Japan continued unopposed as her armies moved into China proper. As Will had predicted, self-interest carried more weight than national honor. Japan may have attacked China to preserve its "national honor," but the real object was to obtain the fertile land in Manchuria.

Soon after the conflict began, Will was on the scene. Early in

November, he began a tour of the Far East to see what was going on.
He visited Mukden, which the Chinese had evacuated:

It is funny what respect and National Honor a few guns will get you ain't it?
China and India, with over half the Population of the world have not only
never been asked to confer, but they have not even been notified what has to
be done with 'em after the other Nations have decided. Yet you give India
and China either Englands navy or ours, and they would not only be invited
to the Conference, they would be the conference. Now we gather to disarm
when a gun has put every Nation in the world where it is today. It all depends
on which end of it you were — the sending or receiving end.[15]

As far as he was concerned, the Japanese aggression represented
another instance of international power politics; although a country
with a large navy and army might not always have the admiration of
the world, it would always be feared and respected.

Rogers visited Manchuria, Japan, Korea, and China; the information he received from war correspondents in the area confirmed what
he already believed. Japan needed more land; and, by virtue of its
superior military strength, it had decided to take Manchuria. The
only other possible expansion area for Japan was to the north in Russian territory, but Russia had an army and China did not. Later,
when the Manchurian affair was brought to the League of Nations,
Will wrote: "Disarmament conference was held up for one hour
while we all went to the League of Nations meeting to demand of
Japan that she quit shooting while the opening session was in conference. The biggest laugh, of course, was uttered unintentionally by
the Japanese when he spoke of Chinese aggression. Well, that like to
broke up the meeting. The conference is off to flying start. There is
nothing to prevent their succeeding now but human nature."[16]

Will not only had little faith in the League of Nations as an instrument for ending the Manchurian conflict, but he also strongly believed that the United States should not become involved in the dispute. Because he recognized the Japanese dedication to "their des-
tiny," he felt that Japan could not be stopped without military action: "The League of Nations is sending here a commission to look
over the ground. That is like a sheriff examining the stall after the
horse disappeared. America could hunt over the world and not find a
better fight to keep out of. There is only two things certain out here,
the Manchurian problem won't be settled this year or next. The sec-

ond certainty is any commission that tries to settle it will wind up in the wrong with both sides."[17]

Rogers' appraisal of the situation was substantiated. By September, 1932, Japan had completed the conquest of Manchuria and had moved into China proper; Shanghai was bombed, and thousands of civilians lost their lives. Although world opinion was aroused, it was too late for effective action. The whole affair confirmed Will's opinion that the Kellogg-Briand Pact was meaningless and the League of Nations ineffective.

III *Philippine Independence*

Will Rogers was a strong advocate of Philippine independence. Soon after World War I, American complacency about its colonial holdings in the Pacific Ocean was shocked by the request of the Filipinos for national independence. Most Americans had assumed that the Filipinos were satisfied with American trusteeship since such a relationship was economically beneficial to the Islanders: they were exempt from restrictive tariff regulations on imports to the United States. A strong spirit of nationalism, however, swept through the islands; and they demanded complete political freedom as guaranteed to them by the Jones Bill of 1916. Public sympathy seemed generally in favor of the proposal, but the inability of Congress to reach a satisfactory severance agreement delayed action.

Will, who became exasperated over the delay, felt that the United States could not afford to void its commitments, however hotly the issue was debated in Congress. When the Hoover administration failed to enact satisfactory legislation, he wrote to the Islanders:

Every Administration since Lincoln has promised you Folks your Liberty, "when you were Ready for it," and you naturally took that Promise serious, well, that will teach you a Lesson the next time. Another thing against you Folks getting your Liberty is the other Nations are against it. If America got out of the Philippines, why, every Native in the Far East would raise a Holler to have England get out of China, out of India, out of the Malay Straits; France out of Indo-China; Japan out of Manchuria and Korea; the Dutch out of Java. In other words, it would be an example in "Freedom for Determination of all Nations" that would shock the world. But we will Stall you off and say you are not ready for it. If your Freedom was left to a Vote of the whole American people you would get it two to one. But anything important is never left to a Vote of the people. We only get to Vote on some man; we never get to Vote on what he is to do. A Delegation of Senators and Congressmen will be the ones to decide just how far advanced you are in Intelligence and how many years away from Freedom, it won't be the people that will do that. So until the American People get some Freedom, why, you Folks can't get any. So, no telling when either one of will be Free.[18]

The humorist had a good reason for wishing the Philippines independent. As his view of the world situation reflected his strong sense of isolationism, so had it also made him a fervent advocate of military preparedness. Since he believed the Philippines could not be defended and might prove a military liability, he saw the islands as a threat to American security if war should come to the Pacific. In 1932, he asserted: "We are going to get into a war someday either over Honolulu or the Philippines. Let's all come home and let every nation ride its own surf-board, play its own eukaleles, and comit their devilment on their own race. Yours for remaining on the home ground."[19]

After his trip to Manchuria in 1932, Will was more and more convinced that the Philippine Islands were a military liability. Sheer distance precluded defending the islands in event of war; and, more important, the Philippines were in the middle of what the humorist once referred to as Japan's "ocean." But Congress again rejected the request by the Philippines for political independence. Will wrote: "Congress yesterday gave forty minutes to Philippine independence, gave forty minutes but no independence. Democrats all voted for it. They are in about the same fix the Philippines are. Sugar and immigration were the things they were voting on. The freedom of a race of people never entered into it. We better give 'em their freedom while we got 'em. The only reason we ever held 'em this long was because Japan didn't use sugar in their tea, but they are liable to start using it any day."[20]

Since defending the Philippines in event of war would cost money which the American taxpayer might be unwilling to appropriate, Rogers believed that the same money, invested in the defense of the homeland, would provide a strong measure of security in a period when the saber-rattling of Hitler, Mussolini, and the Japanese war lords was being heard throughout the world. Consequently, the action of the Roosevelt administration in 1932, which extended the United States guardianship over the Philippines for twelve more years, suited Will not at all. He felt that Congress had yielded to American investors in the Philippines and that it had ignored the wishes of most American citizens. He bitterly commented: "The U.S. Senate sentenced the Philippines to twelve more years of American receivership. How can one nation tell when another nation is ready for independence? But our government can do it. Yes sir, there is not a dozen of 'em thats ever been west of the Golden Gates, but they just could tell you to the day twelve years from now, just when the 'little brown brothers' would be able to mess up their affairs as bad as ours."[21]

IV *War Clouds and Disarmament*

The United States in the decade following World War I had displayed a steady drift toward isolationism. The war had been a disillusioning experience; and a majority of Americans, including Will Rogers, began to feel that the United States had made a mistake in interfering in European affairs. The feeling became more pronounced after the Manchurian situation; more and more the newspapers and national magazines played up the need for America to avoid entanglements with the rest of the world. The younger generation of the late 1920's and early 1930's seemed to be imbued with the psychology of isolationism.

Always a strong advocate of military preparedness, Will had become alarmed during the postwar period when military appropriations were cut to a bare minimum by an economy-minded Congress. Such economy made no sense to him, particularly since aviation was severely curtailed. He wrote:

We better start doing something about our defense. We are not going to be lucky enough to fight Nicaragua forever. Build all we can, and we will never have to use it. . . . All we got to go by is History, and History don't record that "Economy" ever won a war. So I believe I would save my money somewhere else even if I had to work a little shorter handed, around the Capitol there. . . . WHEN WE NEARLY LOSE THE NEXT WAR, AS WE PROBABLY WILL, WE CAN LAY IT ONTO ONE THING AND THAT WILL BE THE JEALOUSY OF THE ARMY AND NAVY TOWARD AVIATION. They have belittled it since it started and will keep on doing it till they have something dropped on them from one.[22]

From Rogers' point of view, as had been observed, the security of a nation rested in no small way upon the size of its army and navy. Through the next five years, Will pounded on the same theme, and pointed to England as an example: "England is a pretty wise old bird.

She relinquished her world's financial supremacy but she didn't relinquish any ships. Shows what she thinks is most important."[23] He seems to have regarded military preparedness as a form of life insurance for national security.

As war threatened in Asia and Europe, Rogers stressed more and more that it was poor economy to cut down on military spending, despite the political value of tax reductions: "Well, lots of war news in the paper today. I knew it was coming when we had cut down on our army and navy. If you want to know when a war is coming, just watch the U.S. and see when they start cutting down on defense. Its the surest barometer in the world."[24] The war news of which Will spoke was focused in Europe where Hitler had repudiated in 1935 the Versailles Treaty and taken Germany out of the League of Nations. England and France were concerned with the militant Nazi movement, which threatened to upset the balance of power in Europe. France rushed the Maginot line to completion. Mussolini had partially mobilized his troops; and the small nations — Rumania, Czechoslovakia, Poland, and Belgium — began negotiations with larger nations for mutual assistance pacts. All of this activity caused Will's remarks in a radio broadcast:

When I had my head turned and wasn't looking on the radio Hitler broke out on me. I thought I had him covered. He tore up the Versailles treaty. It wasn't a good treaty but it was the only one they had. They was years making it and he tore it up in about a minute. . . . England sent its delegation to talk with Mr. Hitler. . . . Hitler talked all day and England didn't know any more when they went home than they did when they got there. . . . Another man named Eden has gone to talk to Russia. . . . No nation likes Russia and all that but they would use them in case of war coming around. . . . they've told Russia "Now you're Communistic, and you believe in dividing up everything. . . . it looks like we're going to have a war over here and we would like to split it with you boys." . . . Well now they'll be coming over here pretty soon. . . . There'll be delegations come and say, "We didn't come to persuade you, or anything, but in case civilization is attacked, why, where do you boys stand?" Well we better say, "If civilization hasn't done any more than it has since the last war, why were again it."[25]

Rogers toured the world again, and his visits to the Far East and Europe convinced him that it was only a question of time before war broke out. His advice to the United States was to stay out of European quarrels. Visiting Austria just a few months after the abortive Nazi putsch, he wrote: "Well, today Austria says they want a gun.

Yesterday it was Germany. Englands got a gun, France has a gun, Italy's got a gun. Germany wants a gun. Austria wants a gun. All God's children want guns, gonna put on the guns, gonna buckle on the guns, and smear up all of God's Heaven."[26]

Returning home, he was more determined than ever that the United States should isolate itself from European affairs. With large oceans on either side, the United States had merely to mind its own business, build a large army and navy, and let the rest of the world take care of itself. As for the pacifists who preached brotherly love as an effective means of preserving peace, Will had this to say: "Brotherly love has never crossed a boundary line yet. If you think it has, why don't somebody protect China. China has never bothered anybody. They have been a friend to the World. They are having their country taken away from 'em, but nobody says a word, for she is so far away that they hope no Nation can march clear through her and get to them. Yes sir, geography has more to do with brotherly love than civilization and Christianity combined."[27] Actually, Will's tendency toward isolationism was more than a reflection of the popular feeling of the time. Although he was an optimist in his daily relationships, he was a confirmed pessimist regarding prospects for a permanent peace. Human nature, he glumly concluded, had not changed; and all the grandiose plans for world peace and world prosperity were useless because of the human element involved.

Will Rogers was a great traveler. Like Mark Twain, he was always on the move; and his search for material for his columns took him around the world three times and to Europe on numerous other occasions. From 1903 to 1904, while still a cowboy, he had worked his way around the world. In vaudeville, he had made several trips to Europe, appearing before audiences in Germany, England, and Ireland. But it was as a columnist and as an unofficial ambassador of the American people that he earned his reputation as a traveler. In the period from 1926 to 1935, he visited almost every country in the world at least once. Rogers' comments on these faraway places show little interest in the scenery of the countries; he was more concerned with the social, political, or economic problems he saw. Since he knew personally more Europeans in high positions than most American diplomats, he conceived it his duty to learn from them the state of affairs in Europe, which he reported through his column to the American people. His view of the world, however, was much like that of the provincial American who sees nothing in a foreign country quite so good as the home grown variety. He had, as Mark Twain had, a fundamental distrust of everything not made in America.

V *England*

Will first visited England in 1902. With his cowboy friend, Dick Paris, he spent seven days in London; and his letters to his family indicate that he was duly impressed with the historical sights of the city. The boys visited the usual tourist attractions, the Houses of Parliament, Buckingham Palace, St. Paul's Cathedral, and Westminster Abbey. He wrote to his father:

Well Dick and I have visited London and find it the biggest case of a town it has ever been my misfortune to find. We visited the House of Parliament where all the great doings of state are carried on, also Buckingham Palace where the King and Queen will reside during the big blowout. . . . Then we went to Westminster Abbey where all the great men of England have monuments erected to their memories, and dumb as I am I felt a curious sensation creep over me while looking at it, although I knew very few of the men personally.[28]

When Will visited London in 1926 as an unofficial ambassador from the United States, his interest largely centered on England's political and economic life. The thing that impressed him most was the fine way that the British met the General Strike which was in progress when he arrived. Over five million men were on strike, but there was no violence, no excitement. There were no pickets, and none of the strikers did anything to interfere with the men who replaced them in a job. As Will put it, the strike should have been called "A Temporary Cession of Employment Without Monetary Consideration for an Indefinite Period, Without Animosity or Hostile Design."[29]

But, if the strike was calm, Rogers found that British politics were not. He visited Parliament when the issue of the strike was being debated; and he was shocked at the conduct of its members. "They are rude in the Commons," he reported. "They holler at each other and interrupt and yell. That's the only ungentlemanly conduct I saw in all England during the strike."[30] The American humorist did not understand the traditional custom in English politics of heckling the opposition. He was amazed that a prominent leader like Lloyd George should be "hooted and hollered at" on the floor of Parliament. He noted, however, that the procedure was effective; for the strike was settled in a few days.

Early in his visit to England, Will met Nancy Astor, the American-born wife of a British peer, who had the distinction of being a member of the House of Commons. Lady Astor knew of Will's interest in British politics and arranged for him to meet some of the leaders of the British Parliament. She wanted me, said Will, to meet her friends and fellow M.P.'s: "This is not meant for Mounted Policemen, as you would naturally interpret it, but it's for Member of Parliament. To be a Mounted Policeman, you have to stand a very rigid examination both mentally and Physically, and serve a very rigid apprenticeship for the position; while with the other M.P.'s there is no requirement necessary."[31]

Will's rural background also made him observant of the farmer's condition in England. Everywhere he went, he observed the way in which British farmers cultivated and cared for their crops. The intensive cultivation of every parcel of land and the way in which it was cared for amazed him. On a trip from Southhampton to London, he wrote, "It's about 80 miles through the most beautiful Country you ever saw up to London; every field planted and plowed, and raising something. And by the way there is no Farm relief problem over here. . . . These fellows looked like they had solved their Farm problems by working on them. . . . You see they have figured out the Jimson weeds and Cockleburs and Sunflowers and all kinds of weeds take up as much room and nourishment out of the ground as wheat and oats do, so they just don't raise them. . . . The trouble with our farmers is that they raise too many things they can't sell."[32]

The highlight of Will's trip was his interview with the Prince of Wales. He had met the Prince in New York the previous year, but now Will was an observer, not an entertainer. The home of the Prince, he remarked, "looked about like an Oil Millionaire's home in Oklahoma, only more simple and in better taste." The Prince "shook hands like a Rotary Club president," and "we talked just like a couple of old Hill Billies." The Prince's room, Will noted, was quite ordinary, with pictures of his brothers and his mother on the mantel. The humorist talked to the Prince about polo and horses; "I didn't ask any questions, I just visited with him. He had a good word for everybody and everything."[33]

Will was also impressed with the English newspapers. He had always said that he only knew what he read in the newspapers, but the English papers provided dull reading. All sensational news of any kind was objectively reported without any lurid details. Crime news appeared in a remote corner of the paper as a statistic: "They won't tell you who was killed, who was robbed, who did the robbing, or any of the details. You can't find out if you had a friend done any good or not. They run it like a baseball box score. You get the results and that is all."[34] The English idea, he reported, is that the police can do more about solving crimes than a newspaper reader can and that a newspaper's job is to report news, not serve as a press agent for a criminal.

Will expressed many times his admiration for British diplomacy. At every peace conference, he noted that the British diplomats seldom made a mistake or a concession. They were always better informed and better prepared than their counterparts from the United States. "England has always been the Daddy of Diplomats," he reported. "The one with the smooth manner . . . he can insult you but he can do it so slick and polite that he will leave you guessing till away after he leaves you whether he was a friend or foe."[35] The success of the British diplomats in comparison to the ineptness of American representatives, explained Will, is because the British regard politics as an obligation and not a business.

England was one of the humorist's favorite countries, for he had a high regard for the government and for its citizens. Since language was no barrier, he made several successful platform appearances in London in his role of entertainer and self-appointed ambassador of goodwill. Employing the same homely manner and sagacious wit which served him so well in the United States, Will gently poked fun at British customs and institutions; and his British audiences responded favorably just as his American audiences did.

VI   *Italy*

When Will went to Italy, he had one objective in mind: to interview Benito Mussolini. The American humorist, like many Americans of his day, had a tremendous admiration for Il Duce, who, he thought, was the greatest man in Europe, and the interview did not disappoint him. He found Mussolini to be a "regular guy" who held down "six cabinet positions" on a salary of "only one thousand dollars a year." He was impressed with the Italian dictator's achievements in government and industry, and with his shrewd appraisal of international diplomacy. Despite his prestige, Will wrote, "I felt as much at home with him as I would with Dinty Moore on 45th street."[36] As to his accomplishments, Will believed that "if he died tomorrow, Italy would always be indebted to him for practically four years of peace and prosperity. Not a bad record for a Guy to die on; but this Guy keeps getting better all the time. He is the only idealist that ever could make it work."[37] The more he read about Mussolini, the more enthusiastic he became. "Dictator form of Government," he wrote, "is the greatest form of Government there is, if you have the right dictator. Well these folks certainly have got him."[38]

Rome as a city did not impress Rogers. Everything had either historical or artistic value, and he had little respect for ancient history or art: "Now we call Rome the seat of culture, but somebody stole the chair." The ruins around the city were uninspiring to Will; he reserved his admiration for the modern plumbing which Mussolini had installed in the new buildings of Rome. He thought the Tiber River was overrated: "Old time history doesn't say a word about the Arkansas, or the South Canadian, or Grand River or the Verdigris, and this here Tiber couldent be a tributary to one of those." The "Collesseum" had been a grand old building, but "they stole enough off it to build everything else in Rome." In fact, said the humorist, "that is why I say there is nothing new here; we got everything over home, only bigger and better."[39]

The historic background of Rome was, however, fascinating to Will. He toured the city and visited virtually all of the ruins and monuments which remained in the city, including the Coliseum, the Forum, and the Catacombs. But as he read about the rise and fall of Rome, he became a bit skeptical of Roman achievement. There is a lot of difference, he said, "between reading something and actually seeing it, for you can never tell till you see it, just how big a liar History is." After visiting the ancient Senate Forum, Will remarked, "I dident know before I got there, and they told me all this — that Rome had Senators. Now I know why it declined."[40]

The great churches and art galleries of Rome apparently made no impression on him. After visiting several of the early Christian churches, he wrote that "Rome has more churches and less preaching in them than any City in the World. Everybody wants to see where Saint Peter was buried. But nobody wants to try and live like him."[41] Since he was primarily interested in living people, Will spent little time in looking at the art exhibited in the museums and churches. In fact, the whole business of rushing from gallery to gallery looking at old masterpieces seemed absurd to him: "In the first place I don't care anything about Oil Paintings. Ever since I struck a dry hole near the old home ranch in Rogers County, Oklahoma, I have hated oil in the raw and all its subsiduaries. You can even color it up, and it don't mean anything to me."[42]

But in Rome it was virtually impossible to avoid art, as Will found out; for, no matter where he might go, he found painting and sculpture. He visited St. Peter's and inspected the Sistine Chapel: "The whole of Rome seems to have been built, painted and decorated by one man; that was Michelangelo. If you took everything out of Rome that was supposed to have been done by Michelangelo, Rome would be as bare of art as Los Angeles."[43] To Rogers, the most fascinating thing about the Sistine Chapel was that Michelangelo had had to paint the ceiling while lying flat on his back. He was also impressed with the variety of talent which Michelangelo possessed: "He was a picture Painter, Sculptor, a House painter both inside and out — for in those days they painted the ceiling. . . . He was an architect, a Landscape Gardner, Interior Decorator, and I wouldent doubt if he dident strum a mean Guitar."[44] The magnitude of the great artist's work also amazed Will as it had amazed Mark Twain before him: "Henry Ford has always received credit for what we call mass production. But I want to tell you that if Michelangelo even turned out all the Statues they say he did — thats even if he dident paint at all — why he was the originator of Mass Production, not Uncle Henry."[45]

The scenic wonders of Italy made no impression upon the humorist. When he visited the Bay of Naples, he wrote, "Did you ever see the harbor of San Francisco? Well it makes the Bay of Naples look like the Chicago drainage canal, and I am from Los Angeles too."[46] After visiting Pompeii, he wrote, "Now if you like buried cities you cant beat this one, personally I dont care for buried cities."[47] In Venice, he remarked,

They rave over Venice; there's nothing there but water. Why, Louisiana has more water in their cellars than the whole Adriatic Sea. And the Grand Canyon — well, I just don't want to hurt their feelings talking about it. No, sir, Europe has nothing to recommend it but its old age, and the Petrified forest in Arizona makes a Sucker out of it for old age. Why, that forest was there and doing business before Nero took his first Violin lesson. You take the Guides and the Grapes out of Europe and she is just a Sahara. It's great for you to see, if somebody is paying for it, or paying you to do it. But just as a pure educational proposition or pastime, it ain't there.[48]

VII   *Russia*

When Will went to Russia in 1926 to see how Communism worked, he hoped to be permitted to travel to the major cities in the Soviet
Union and perhaps interview some of the Russian leaders. Unfortunately, his movements were restricted; and he was not permitted to
interview either Stalin or Trotsky. But he did gain some ideas on the
problems of the Communist government for he was permitted to interview some minor officials and to visit with a number of American
Communists then living in Moscow. From what they told him, he
was able to make some shrewd guesses as to the reason why he was
not permitted to see Trotsky: "But I found out the real reason I dident get to see Trotsky. Trotsky is not in so good with the present
government. It may seem rather funny to some to hear he is too conservative for them. . . ."[49]

Will was astute enough to recognize the struggle for power which
was being waged in the Kremlin. The power which Lenin had controlled as the first leader of the United Soviet Socialists' Republic
was gradually being shifted into the hands of Josef Stalin:

The real fellow that is running the whole thing in there is a bird named Stalin,
a great big two-fisted egg from away down in the Caucasian Mountains. He
is the Borah of the Black Seas. He is kinder the Mellon and Butler combined
of the Russian administration. He is the stage manager of Bolshevism right
now. He don't hold any great high position himself but he tells the others
what ones they will hold. . . . Well, Trotsky is kinder not sitting at his round
table for lunch. But the peasants out in the country are still strong for
Trotsky. . . . he is called a conservative. A conservative among the Communists is a man with a Bomb in only one hand; a Radical is what you would
call a Two-Bomb man. . . .[50]

The Communist experiment interested Will. Trying to learn
something about the political system of the Soviet Union, he asked
many questions and received many answers. Explanations were volu-
ble enough, but they made no sense to him. "One thing a Communist
can do is explain," he said. "You ask him any question in the world
and if you give him long enough he will explain their angle, and it will
sound plausible then. Communism to me is one-third practice and
two-thirds explanation."[51]

A year later when the power struggle between Stalin and Trotsky was resolved with the expulsion of Trotsky from the Soviet Union, Will wrote:

Russia has thrown Trotsky out. There is a funny thing about Trotsky. I was over there last summer and found out He is too conservative. This Bird Stalin that is the male Mussolini of Russia, he and Trotsky don't gee together. You see a Conservative in Russia is a fellow that thinks you only ought to divide with him what you have, while a real communist believes that you ought to give it all to him, in exchange you get to call him Comrade. But you notice they don't do any banishing to Siberia, or promiscuous shooting with him. They would like too but they don't dare. You know he and Lenin started in together and while Lenin is dead, the old Peasants still are strong for Trotzky, so no matter how mad the ruling party might get you can go and bet they will never harm Trotzky. He stands too good with the old farmers. He knows a lot of these things they are trying is apple sauce, and won't work. Communism is like Prohibition, it's a good idea but it won't work.[52]

As far as Will could tell, there was no real change in the class system in the Soviet Union. The Russian people were just like other people of the world: "People dont change under Government, the governments change but the people remain the same. . . . Russia under the Czar was very little different from what it is today; for instead of one Czar, why, there is àt least a thousand now. . . . Siberia is still working. It's just as cold on you to be sent there under the Soviets as it was under the Czar. . . . They are all supposed to only receive $112 a month, which is supposed to be the salary of all Communists that do work for the Government. Well, some of them must be pretty good managers to get along as well as they do on that."[53]

In the two weeks that he spent in Russia, Will traveled to most of the major industrial centers of the Soviet Union. In Moscow, he found a group of American expatriates who were in Russia under the leadership of William Haywood, a labor leader who had been active in the formation of the radical labor organization known as the Industrial Workers of the World. Will tried to see Haywood to get his impressions of conditions among the industrial workers in Russia. He wrote: ". . . also met all the gang they sent out from America that time with Big Bill Haywood — was going to see old Bill but he was sick in the Hospital and I couldent get to see him. From what I heard, Bill would sho like to get back among the gang from Chicago."[54]

Will visited at great length with these exiled Americans. He found that all of them were enthusiastic about the Russian experiment; however, he also sensed among them an uneasiness about their own positions. Although they praised the Russian leaders and spoke glowingly about the conditions of Russian workers, he noticed that they took great care to keep their American passports handy. After talking to the group, Rogers reported: "The funny part about it among all these American ones you meet over here visiting, they are all so nice and friendly and enthusiastic about it — Communism — and believe in it away above our form of government; but they all go back home. It just looks to me like Communism is such a happy family affair that not a Communist wants to stay where it is practiced. It's the only thing they want you to have but keep none for themselves."[55]

Before going to the Soviet Union, Will had made every effort to learn something about the Communistic theory so that he might have a basis for judging the success of the system. He read some books which described the Communist experiment, including some articles by Karl Marx; and he talked with several Russian experts in the United States. "I am not criticising," wrote Will, "but I have come to the conclusion that the reason there is so many books on Socialism is because it's the only thing in the world that you can't explain easy. It is absolutely impossible for any Socialist to say anything in a few words. You say 'Is it light or dark' and it takes him two volumes to answer Yes or No; and then I know there is a catch in it somewhere. . . . If Socialists worked as much as they talked, they would be the most prosperous Government in the World."[56]

Everywhere he went, Will found evidence of the difficulties which Russia was having in producing and marketing consumer goods. Shop windows and shelves were empty of everything except the bare necessities. Food was expensive despite the cooperative stores which were designed to keep prices down for the average citizen. Taxes were high, and the farmers were unhappy and uncooperative. The only items that seemed to be in abundant supply were the propaganda posters exalting the virtues of the Soviet leaders and exhorting the workers to great effort for the state. Everywhere there were museums and exhibitions displaying pictures and relics of the Revolution. After visiting the Revolutionary Museum in Leningrad, Will wrote:

Communism will never get anywhere till they get the basic idea of Propaganda out of their head and replace it with some work. If they plowed as much as they Propagandered, they would be richer than the Principality of Monaco. The trouble is they got all their theorys out of a book instead of any of them ever going to work and practicing them. I read the same books these Birds learned from and that's the books of that guy Marx. Why he was like one of these efficiency experts. He could explain to you how you could save a million dollars and he couldent save enough himself to eat on.[57]

Will was tremendously impressed with the Soviet development of air power. In the United States, he had always advocated a stronger emphasis on military aviation and had warned of the consequences which such neglect might produce in a time of war. Now in Russia he saw considerable evidence of the Soviet Union's concern for developing strength in air power. He warned, "You had better start doing something in aviation in the United States. The Russians are sure a doing it here . . . the next war you dont want to Look Out; you want to Look Up. When you look up and see a cloud during the next war to end wars, don't you be starting to admire its silvery lining till you find out how many Junkers and Fokkers are hiding behind it."[58] Moreover, as the humorist noted, the emphasis in Soviet Russia was on military rather than on commercial aircraft. By way of a reminder, Will added, "Nobody is walking but us, everybody else is flying. So in a few years when somebody starts dropping on us, don't you say I didn't tell you."[59]

Will could not tell whether or not the Russian people were contented under the Communist regime. He walked the streets in Moscow and Leningrad and talked through an interpreter to a large number of Soviet citizens. They seem content, he wrote, but then the Russians are naturally sad people: "I may be wrong about these people, for you can never tell about a Russian. They all may be just having the best time in the World over here and enjoying it all fine. You know, that is one thing about a Russian — he thrives on adversity. He is never so happy in his life as when he is miserable. So he may just be setting pretty, for he is certainly miserable. It may be just the land for a Comrade to want to hibernate in."[60]

In 1934, when Will made another visit to Russia, he traveled from East to West, taking the Trans-Siberian railway from Vladivostok to Moscow. Moscow had changed greatly since his last visit. Despite the world-wide depression, the Soviet Union had undertaken a vast construction project to house the growing population of Moscow. The humorist was impressed with the number and size of the buildings: "They are building thousands of apartments for the people. They are four, five, and six stories high. Yet I never saw a fire escape in Russia. I asked 'em how they was going to get down, and they said, they never thought of that. No elevators either in the apartment houses. . . . Looks like they are constructed pretty cheaply. Well they are in such a hurry to get 'em up and care for the people, that they just throw 'em together the best they can."[61]

Will traveled from Moscow down the Ukraine. As was his custom, he talked to Russian officials, American newspaper correspondents, and the people he met on the streets. Russia is a country that can answer everybody's questions, said Will, "Do you want to hear that it is terrible? Well it is. Do you want to hear that they are all working and making some sort of a living? Well they are. . . . You can get any kind of answer in Russia that you want to. . . . Now to get any kind of idea of Russia, everything we do, every viewpoint we have, every matter of fact way of looking at anything is entirely different in Russia. I was surprised they didn't walk on their hands instead of their feet, just to be different from capitalistic nations."[62]

But, as on all of Will's trips, he was primarily interested in people. With an interpreter, he stopped and talked with as many Soviet citizens as he could. He attended a Writers Conference in Moscow and listened to speech after speech extolling the literary genius of Maxim Gorky. He talked with Morris Hindus, Walter Duranty, and Louis Fischer — all correspondents who had lived in Russia for several years. But the Soviet condition still remained an enigma to the humorist: "The main question everybody asks me is — are they happy. That's a tough one to answer. There are millions of people in Russia. I couldn't talk their language so I couldn't ask them are you happy? It's awful hard to look at a person and tell just how happy they are. . . . We'd see people coming down to the trains and just stand there. They'd just be standing at the station with a dull, blank expression on their faces — no joy, no smile. . . . And then, too, here's what everybody tells me, the Russians are naturally sad people. That they don't feel good until something's really the matter with them. In other words a Russian ain't happy til he's hurt. So to answer the question 'is Russia happy?' I should answer yes for they've certainly got enough the matter with them to make them happy."[63]

During the next year, the humorist made another trip to Russia, but there was never a fundamental change in his attitude toward Communism. The Marxist philosophy was alien to the frontier spirit of the cowboy humorist, and he could never condone or understand the regimentation of the Soviet system. He was suspicious of the idealistic principles and slogans of the Soviet experiment and distrustful of the motives of the Soviet leaders.

VIII *Mexico and Central America*

Of all the countries in the western hemisphere, Will had an especial fondness for Mexico. Perhaps it was because of his Cherokee Indian heritage which recognized a kinship with the Indians in Mexico. At any rate, from the beginning of his career as a political humorist, he reacted strongly and positively in championing Mexico in its relationship with American investors and with the United States. He staunchly defended, as has been observed, Mexican rights in the dispute over mineral rights; praised Mexican culture; and encouraged Mexican development of its own national resources. For example, during the Coolidge administration, the United States became involved in a dispute with the Mexican government over claims of private American investors. When Secretary Kellogg sent a note to the Mexican government supporting American claims and pointedly saying that the eyes of the world were on Mexico, Will commented caustically:

Now what Ye Old Reliable Illiterate Digest wants to know is what the devil business is it of ours how some other country runs its business. How does Kellogg or Coolidge know what the EYES OF THE WORLD ARE ON? As a matter of fact the eyes of the world are on a $1 bill and especially if somebody else has it. Outside of the Oil Interests and Americans who want to make money out of Mexico, the rest of the world doesn't even know that Mexico exists (and incidentally Mexico is not worrying about them). There is only one way to prevent war, and that is FOR EVERY NATION TO TEND TO ITS OWN BUSINESS.[64]

In 1927, diplomatic relations between the United States and Mexico came near the breaking point. The old "dollar diplomacy" policy no longer worked well, and the new administration in Mexico under President Calles talked threateningly of expropriating American oil and mineral properties. Alarmed, American investors appealed to the Federal government for support; and some fanatics even talked wildly about military action against Mexico. There was an exchange of diplomatic notes, but these, as well as meetings between representatives of both governments, had little effect.

To ease the tension, President Calvin Coolidge appointed his old friend Dwight D. Morrow as Ambassador to Mexico with instructions to deal directly with the elected representatives of the Mexican government and not with the vested groups in Mexico. To help on his initial assignment, Ambassador Morrow, in an effort to seek good will for his mission, invited Will Rogers and Charles Lindbergh to come to Mexico with him. As the first man to fly the Atlantic, Charles Lindbergh was an international hero; as for Will Rogers, the invitation was welcome in as much as it made semi-official his self-assumed title of "unofficial ambassador of good will for the United States."

Will acknowledged the invitation in a pretended letter to President Coolidge. "My dear Calvin," he began,

Well I just got down here as you suggested me doing. You said I ought to go somewhere, so I figured it was Mexico. . . . We've started to pay some attention to our neighbors on the south. Up to now our calling card to Mexico or Central America has been a gunboat or a bunch of violets shaped like Marines. We could never understand why Mexico wasent just crazy about us; for we always had their good-will, and Oil and coffee and minerals at heart. Of course, as you know up there, Mr. President, some were just for going down and taking Mexico over. Where did this country down here, with no great chains of Commercial Clubs and Chambers of Commerce and Junior and Freshmen Chambers of Commerces and Rotary and Kiwanis and Lions and Tiger Clubs, and no Golf pants, and no advertising Radio programs — where did a Nation like that come in to have Oil anyway. It was kind of an imposition on their part to even have to go to the trouble of going down and taking their country over.[65]

Ambassador Morrow's first visit to Mexico was a successful one. He made a two-week train tour through the country with President Calles, and he generally ignored the overtures of the vested-interest groups, including the aristocracy. When Will arrived, he was taken immediately to the palace to meet President Calles. At this time, the political situation was rather tense; for, in the recent election, several presidential candidates had been assassinated. At the introduction, Will made a gesture of surrender. "Tell this Bird," Will said, "Make it perfectly clear to him that I am just down here for fun. I am not a candidate for anything."[66] At the audaciousness of the remark, Morrow blanched, but Calles roared with laughter. Morrow later remarked that this "impertinence" broke the formality of the occasion and made it possible for him to deal with Calles on a personal basis.

Will traveled for several days with the presidential party visiting the interior of Mexico where he was shown the power dams, the farm co-operatives, and the agricultural stations which were sponsored by the government. When the party returned to Mexico City, the humorist was invited to a reception in the Chapultepec Castle, the home of the President, and later was taken to observe a session of the Chamber of Deputies. Of the experience, he wrote, "Oh, we went into their Congress. They call it the Chamber of Deputies, and they wear pistols. They are allowed to wear a Gun the same as an officer. I got a big kick out of that. . . . I kinder like it. I never heard one Deputy call another a Liar all the time I watched 'em operate. But up home it has become so common that it's almost a greeting."[67]

Ambassador Morrow honored Will with a dinner at the American Embassy. President Calles was invited and accepted the invitation. It was the first time in history that the chief executive of Mexico had entered the American Embassy. After remarks by the dignitaries present, Will was called up to deliver what he referred to as an impromptu speech "that I only worked on steady for about four days."[68] After his usual barbed comments that punctured the dignity of the diplomats present, he gave some sagacious advice to the Mexican people:

Now I want it distinctly understood that I dident come down here to try and cement good relations between the two Nations. . . . I am not going to tell you that you ought to wake up and be progressive and trade your Burro for a car. The only thing I see that you need in this Country is more rain, and if Calles here don't give it to you, I would start impeachments. I dident come here to tell you that Mexico needed American Capital. Mexico needs Mexican Capital. Pass a law to make your rich Mexican invest at least half the money he gets out of his own country back into it again. You have more money in this city invested in French dresses and perfumes than you have in the country in Plows. It's not American confidence that you are looking for — it's Mexican confidence.[69]

The Mexican trip was a great experience for Will, and it was beneficial for the United States government as well. Everywhere the humorist went, he found good-natured applause and appreciation. His championship of Mexican rights to develop their own natural resources and his open expression of his admiration for the Mexican people did a great deal to break down the fear and mistrust which many Mexican nationals were beginning to feel toward the United States.

All of the countries south of the border fascinated Will. In 1931, he planned a trip which would take him through Central America to Guatemala, Costa Rica, Nicaragua, and Panama. He was particularly interested in Nicaragua whose sovereignty he had defended as far back as 1926 when President Coolidge had sent the United States Marines into that tiny country during a political dispute "to protect American lives and property." At that time Will had written, "We send Marines to Nicaragua to tell them how to run an election and send missionaries to China. No wonder we are funny to the rest of the world."[70]

A week before Will was scheduled to depart on his tour, a disastrous earthquake struck Nicaragua that virtually destroyed the city of Managua and left thousands of people hungry and homeless. Will rushed directly to the scene of the tragedy and was appalled by the conditions which he found there. He personally gave five thousand dollars to the Red Cross for the relief fund and appealed through his daily column to the American people for additional aid: "Here is some divine spark of relief for the anti-prohibitionists. Everything in town was destroyed but the brewery. Churches, schools, banks, stores all went." But it was an act of providence, he wrote, "for the water works were destroyed and all they had to drink was beer. . . . Now they need money and help."[71]

Will then toured Central America putting on benefit shows to raise money for the stricken city. On his tour, he stopped in Panama where he found the Panamanians up in arms over some undiplomatic remarks made by Senator Bookhart of Iowa during a recent visit to the country. The senator had been highly critical of the social conditions in Panama, and his speech had aroused the resentment of both the Panamanians and the Americans living there. Newspapers were demanding a public apology, and there was talk of making a formal complaint to Washington. When Will arrived, the situation was explained to him by Roy T. Davis, minister to Panama; and the humorist was asked to do what he could to dispel the unpleasant incident.

That evening Will gave a benefit performance in Panama City for the earthquake victims at Managua. Donald Day describes the scene as follows:

As Will shuffled to the center of the stage, the hostility of the audience could be felt. "Well folks," Will drawled, "All I know is what I read in the newspapers, you know. . . . I read what our Senator said about you 'Wallowing in Sin.' . . . Just as soon as I read that I hopped in a plane and flew to Panama. . . . I thought if you was 'wallowing in sin,' why I'd ask you to move over and I'd wallow with you." There was a moment of silence and a roar of laughter swept through the audience, most of whom understood English. In one bold thrust, Will had swept away all the resentment of the senator's crabbed speech with a good cleansing dose of laughter. . . .[72]

Despite the amount of traveling Will did, or the foreign countries he visited, he was always glad to return home. To him, America was God's country, and he never let his readers forget it. He himself was thoroughly American, and nothing that Europe, Asia, or South America had to offer could compare to his homeland: the art, culture, and history of Europe made no impression on him; he found the social and economic experiment of Communism to be distasteful; and he was appalled at the low standard of living in Japan, Korea, and China. His broad humanitarian and religious tolerance embraced all men and all creeds, but his patriotism was reserved for, and expressed in, an unashamed pride in American institutions.

Throughout his long career as a public commentator, Will Rogers remained fairly consistent in the themes which he expressed in his columns. He never deviated from his opposition to entangling foreign alliances, his abhorrence of religious bigotry, his dislike of partisan politics, and his support of American institutions. But there is a contradiction, or inconsistency, in his basic attitudes toward some of these themes. Thus it is difficult to reconcile Will's fervent admiration for Mussolini with his resentment toward warmongers and international power politicians, or his strong isolationist feelings as against equally strong anti-imperialistic views. These inconsistencies are the more surprising in that Will himself apparently never recognized them as contradictory, and never tried to justify them.

Will's admiration for Mussolini was expressed as early as 1926, after he had interviewed Il Duce in Rome, and as late as 1933, when he wrote, "Say Mussolini could run this country with his eyes shut, in fact that is the way our Congress has been running it."[73] Soon after his first enthusiastic eulogy of Mussolini appeared in print, Gilbert Seldes took the humorist to task for his evaluation. After praising Rogers as a comedian, Seldes added, "But when he takes to quoting long political essays on the nobility of the Fascist 'castor oil treatment'; when he discusses international affairs, not for their yield of wise-cracks, but for their inherent bearing — he becomes a little, lost child."[74] Will Rogers, Jr., believes that his father's attitude toward Mussolini was the result of his failure to look beyond the facade of the dictatorial form of government to see its methods of operation; Will simply accepted the end as justifying the means, for he saw the modernization of Italian industry and government as a sign of progress without investigating the manner in which these reforms were made. In this respect, the humorist did not differ from many Americans who accepted Mussolini's modern plumbing, paving of highways, and running trains on time as evidence of the efficiency of the Fascist system but who ignored the inherent social and political evils of the dictator-directed state.

Will's isolationism carried within it the seeds of an intense nationalism. Popular sentiment in the United States after World War I had reacted against the idea of international idealism and the related idea of American responsibility in international affairs. The humorist shared with many Americans the belief in the superiority and self-sufficiency of the United States. Paradoxically, however, Will was an equally intense anti-imperialist and a humanitarian, firmly convinced of the natural right of all people of the world to self-determination, as his columns on China and Mexico will testify. Like other anti-imperialists before him, Rogers seems to have believed that imperialist aims ran counter to the dictates of common sense, economic interests, and moral well-being. However, Will was not an intellectual, nor a student of social and political theory; and his attitude toward isolationism and anti-imperialism was likely to be conditioned by the political and social climate of his time. Moreover, Rogers' frontier background may account in part for his democratic belief in self-determination, as well as his distrust of things not American.

Yet these inconsistencies merely confirm Will's position as spokesman for the people since many Americans apparently shared his seemingly contradictory views. On most issues, he took the middle ground along with a majority of his readers. In few areas could the humorist be classified as a liberal, but neither could he be tagged as a conservative. He was suspicious of intellectuals; but, at the same time, he was proud to count many of them, such as Will Durant, Walter Lippmann, and H. L. Mencken, as friends. New ideas and new theories he was willing to accept, but usually with reservation. On several occasions, he took the unpopular side of controversial issues — for example the General Billy Mitchell court-martial — but generally he was content to express pungently what millions of his readers were vaguely thinking. Sometimes he was right, sometimes he was wrong, and sometimes he contradicted himself; but it made no difference, for to his readers he was always in the main stream of American thought and history.

CHAPTER 5

The Anatomy of Will's Humor

ONE of the problems in discussing Will Rogers' technique of humor is keeping in mind that we are dealing with two personalities: Will, the professional humorist, and Will, the man. However, unlike Charles Farrar Browne, Finley Peter Dunne, and other nineteenth-century humorists· whose characters contrasted *greatly* in personality with their creators, Will was *virtually* the same in private life as he was before the public eye. Outwardly his trademarks were chewing gum and twirling ropes, and these were as characteristic of his off-stage manner as his rumpled suits and tousled forelock. His Oklahoma drawl was a natural one, as was his manner of expressing himself in the pungent metaphors and rude colloquialisms of the West. At home, he was as casual and relaxed as he appeared on the stage; and his non-professional recreations were riding and roping, which were entirely in keeping with his professional character as a former cowboy.

Yet there was a significant difference between Will Rogers as a performer and as a private citizen — his pretense as the former that he was an ignorant and illiterate fellow who had no education and who knew only what he read in the newspapers. This pretense was apparently adopted by the humorist early in his career when he achieved success in vaudeville as a cowboy philosopher; his audiences were delighted with the incongruity between his pretended ignorance and his common-sense remarks. At the same time, Will seems to have discovered that, by playing the "fool character," he could say and write things that would have been resented by the public if expressed as an intellectual. Because of this pose, the public accepted the humorist as a kind of court jester who was permitted liberties denied to the more serious political commentators.

Actually, Will Rogers was neither ignorant nor illiterate. In Indian Territory, he had received the equivalent of a high school education;

and his continued reading of books and newspapers made him a well-informed man. His letters to his family, written when he was working in South Africa in 1902, show little of the ungrammatical nature of his later humorous writing. Two reasons exist for Will's ungrammatical style: first, during his early years in vaudeville, he found it an effective vehicle for his humor; second, although he recognized the ungrammatical structure of his writing and speaking, he hesitated to tamper with success. Over a period of time, he standardized and habitually used the vernacular as his regular expression both in public and private life.

On occasions Will, himself, demonstrated that his pretense of ignorance was a pose. When several letters appeared in the newspapers questioning his knowledge of politics and foreign affairs, he wrote:

Everybody sure was "Jumpy" during this late uprising. . . . For instance they would write to the paper, "I read Will Rogers, but why does he have to dabble in Politics. Let him stay on the funny stuff where he belongs." Well if they would just stop to think I have written on nothing but Politics for years. . . . I have been in almost every country in the last few years. I have talked with prominent men of those countrys, our Ambassadors or Ministers, and I would have to be pretty dumb to not soak up some information. . . . Where do these other fellows get all of their vast store of knowledge? I never hear of em going any place. If I write about Mexico, I have been down there half a dozen times. There is not a state in this Country that I am not in every once in a while. . . . Now I read Politics, talk Politics, know personally almost every prominent Politician, like em and they are my friends, but I cant help it if I have seen enough of it to know that there is some *baloney* in it. . . . I am going to call em as I see em. If I dont see things your way, well, why should I. . . . Politics is the best show in America and I am going to keep on enjoying it.[1]

Will's often repeated dictum, "All I know is what I read in the newspapers," was another part of his posture of ignorance. As has been already stated, he did read the newspapers avidly, and daily news items were a major source of humor; moreover, he tried to read several different newspapers in order to get opposing points of view about the news. He once wrote, "If you are going to write, talk, comment, or argue over any public question, dont do it by reading just one newspaper. I try to get all kinds, breeds, creeds, and every single different political one."[2] However, his knowledge of world affairs was amplified through his friendships with prominent business men and political leaders who talked to him freely about problems of both national and international concern. He also read books and periodicals whenever he found it expedient to expand his understanding of a particular issue or problem. Newspapers may have been the major source of his knowledge about the world, but there were other sources which he also used.

Will's seemingly casual manner of expressing his humor was another part of his pose. Most of his jokes appeared to be spontaneous; yet, as in any form of art, a good deal of hard work was necessary. Although he wrote hurriedly, he took considerable pains with his daily column, fussing and worrying to get it exactly right. Often he expressed an idea in several ways before he got a sentence that suited him. A staff writer from the *New Republic*, on visiting the humorist's dressing room at the Follies, made this observation: "In the typewriter, on this occasion, was a sheet of paper on which were written seven or eight version of the same quip, each an improvement on the one before. In the performance, he did his monologue with the lariat. In the middle of it, he stopped, chuckled as though a thought had suddenly struck him at that minute, and repeated the final version of the joke verbatim."[3] Rogers put forth considerable effort to make his humorous ideas appear to be effortless and accidental, and his success in this pose testifies to his boundless industry and his native wit.

Despite this pose of ignorance and studied carelessness, the personalities of Will the humorist and Will the man were not too far apart. Probably his readers gave little thought to the distinction; they seem to have accepted him as an average American who had been born with a good deal of common sense, who had never had a formal education to distort his thinking, and who had become exceptionally wise in figuring out simple solutions for the complex problems of life. These qualities made Rogers a humorist and a philosopher, and he could not drop them completely in passing from the public stage to private life. There are a good many illiterate people who look and talk as Will Rogers did, but he became unique as a wit because his mental equipment was far beyond that of the average man. When the humorist remarked that all he knew was what he read in the newspapers, he was simply attesting to the legitimacy of his role as a homespun, one hundred percent, no-nonsense-about-me, American humorist. Wittingly or unwittingly, he was testifying to his authentic descent from the line of Josh Billings, Petroleum V. Nasby, Artemus Ward, and Mark Twain.

Will's early humor was developed during his career on the variety stage of New York, and it reflected, for the most part, the viewpoint of the vaudeville comedian. Among New Yorkers the stock character of the "yokel" was always a source of humor; thus the apparent illiteracy of the cowboy philosopher enhanced his stage personality. The common-sense nature of his pronouncements made in this rural idiom provided an element of incongruity which his audiences found irresistible. In addition, his inimitable drawl and infectious grin helped establish him as a stage personality.

In 1922, when Will became a columnist, writing became the principal outlet for his humor. In the transition from oral to written humor, Rogers carried with him the same devices, mannerisms, and pretenses. Although he could not transfer his grin and his drawl to the printed page, he employed in his written work the same homely and colorful mode of expression, the same characteristic qualities of simplicity and directness, and the same pretense of ignorance and illiteracy.

I. *Style*

The form of Will's writing is difficult to classify. His daily column was generally a short expository paragraph seldom exceeding two hundred words. Written as a daily telegram and sent from wherever the humorist might be at the time, the material exhibits a stenographic terseness with connectives often omitted; and, since the thought is greatly compressed, the column often gives an impression of simplicity and informality. The column is almost always written in the first person; and the humorist sometimes is merely reporting, but more often he is editorializing on the news. The short article was always printed just as it was received with no attempt made to correct spelling, grammar or punctuation.

As a result of his commitment to a daily column, Will always traveled with his portable typewriter at his side. His columns were apt to be written anywhere: on an airplane, in a restaurant, at the telegraph office, or even in the back seat of his car. He would thumb through the newspapers, read an article here and there, and occasionally mark an item with a stub pencil. When an idea came to mind, he would turn to the typewriter and peck away, always in capital letters. Now and then he would stop and read what he had written; then start again. Often he would read the article to someone to watch the reaction. If the reaction was unfavorable, he would rephrase the column or try a new idea. Then the dispatch was sent to the telegraph office, and his writing commitment was over for the day.

The weekly column, which appeared each Sunday, was much longer, averaging about twenty-five hundred words. Digressions were frequent in the weekly column, and often the article seemed to be merely a series of short paragraphs tied together with little transition between the humorous ideas. Sometimes the column was devoted to one subject; sometimes several newsworthy items would appear. Although the fundamental form was expository and in the first person, Will varied the pattern to suit his purpose. The column sometimes took the form of a letter to one of his critics; at other times, it appeared to be an interview with an official of the government; on several occasions it was presented in the form of comedy drama.

Will was extremely conscientious in fulfilling his obligation to write both a daily and a weekly article for the syndicate. Only on rare occasions did he miss filing his material; and once, when he was sent to the hospital for major surgery, the last thing he did before the operation was to dictate three daily articles in advance. He undoubtedly tired of the daily stint although his wife, Betty Rogers, wrote that, "when he really got into the swing of things, these daily pieces became his favorite medium. In later years he would have been glad to drop the weekly articles; but doing a daily wire, though it might sometimes be difficult, was never drudgery. So from October 15, 1926 on, Will sent in his wire every day, six days a week, no matter where he was or what he was doing."[4]

Since Will's columns presented his own views and attitudes, the McNaught syndicate had difficulty when his articles presented a different opinion from the editorial policy of the syndicated newspapers in which his column appeared. The newspapers could omit a column which ran counter to editorial policy, but such was Will's popularity that the public objected strenuously when a column was missing. Will would not tolerate censorship of his material by the syndicate or the newspapers; as a result, the *New York Times,* when one of his columns took a stand on the issue of war debts which was contrary to the paper's position, ran an editorial pointing out that Will's opinions were his own and did not represent the editorial policy of the paper. Will responded as follows: "I would like to state to the readers of the *New York Times* that I am in no way responsible for the editorial policy of this paper. I allow them free reign as to their opinion, so long as its within the bounds of good subscription gathering. But I want it distinctly understood that their policy may be in direct contrast to mine. Their editorials may be put in purely for humor, or just to fill space. Every paper must have its various entertaining features and not always to be taken seriously, and never to be construed as my policy."[5]

Will's books do not have any structural pattern. All of his books except one, *Ether and Me,* were collections of humorous material previously used by the cowboy philosopher either on the stage or in his column. His first two publications, *The Cowboy Philosopher on the Peace Conference* and *The Cowboy Philosopher on Prohibition,* are nothing more than a series of jokes which he had previously used in the Ziegfeld Follies; the quips are presented as paragraph units; and they are bound together only by concern for a common theme. The *Peace Conference* concerns President Woodrow Wilson's efforts to secure the adoption of his Fourteen Points and the diplomatic maneuverings among the Allied nations in preparing the Versailles treaty. The book on Prohibition is basically a humorous attack on the prohibitionists and the Volstead Enforcement Act. His third book, *The Illiterate Digest,* is a collection of his weekly columns for book publication, and the subjects range from the Tea Pot Dome political scandal to Will's comments on etiquette.

One of his most popular books was *Letters of a Self-Made Diplomat to His President,* a collection of articles written for the *Saturday Evening Post;* the articles are structurally related by their form, for the book purports to be a series of letters written to President Calvin Coolidge that describe Will's observations during his tour of Europe in 1926. In addition to describing the general European scene, the humorist sends advice to Coolidge about the farm problem and on the Congressional election of 1926. On the same trip, Will made his first visit to Russia, and *There is Not a Bathing Suit in Russia* is an account of this trip. *Ether and Me* is a short volume describing a gall-stone operation which Will underwent in 1929. Other than these books and his columns, Will's writing was confined to a few magazine articles, generally on political subjects, and to the introductions to books written by such friends as Eddie Cantor and Charles Russell.

On the lecture platform, Will used many of the same devices of humor which had served him so well in his columns and in his vaudeville routines. Strolling onto the stage dressed in a rumpled blue serge suit, wearing a broad grin on his face, chewing gum in his mouth, and presenting an air of unpretentious informality, he spoke in his characteristic southwestern drawl; and he began his performance slowly as if he were trying to gauge the mood of the audience. He always began with jokes about such local problems as the city council, bootlegging, traffic problems, bond issues and city elections; he got this material from talking to friends, reading the newspapers, and speaking to reporters about community affairs. He mentioned the names of local personalities, usually innocuous jests about the mayor, the chief of police, and the superintendent of schools. After the audience had been warmed up with comments about local affairs, Will turned to the state political scene, gently ridiculing the governor and state legislature. Finally, he tackled national and international problems, which he called his "sure fire stuff." This part of his lecture was similar to his columns; he commented both humorously and sagaciously on newsworthy items of the nation or the world.

Although Will prepared copious notes before his lectures, he never referred to them during his performance; and his material seemed completely spontaneous and original. How long he talked depended on how the audience responded to his jokes. If the audience was particularly enthusiastic, he talked well beyond the allotted time. As he talked, he moved about the platform, stopping to lean against the podium, lounging on a piano bench, and sometimes sitting on the edge of the platform with his legs dangling over. The homespun manner in which he spoke and the common-sense pronouncements which he made brought him in close rapport with almost every audience.

II *Grammar*

In keeping with his pose of ignorance, Will's language, in both his written and oral expression, was nonliterary, to say the least. It may be termed a homely, low-colloquial expression characterized by misspellings, grammatical errors, weak punctuation, and excessive slang. The humorist seems to have written carelessly, almost slovenly at times, with a fine disregard for the rules of grammar, preferring to believe that it was his thought and his ideas that made his humor and not his manner of expression. Some of his most common errors were subject-verb-agreement, improper case, incorrect number or gender, misplaced modifiers, improper tense formation, and sentence fragments.

Some of Will's grammatical errors appear so frequently that they appear to be individual irregularities which characterize his style. For example, his sentence structure was often loose and inept; for he wrote exactly as he spoke, without any attempt to subordinate elements of his sentences. Thus his most common sin of punctuation was the run-on sentence; when he came to the end of a complete thought, he simply inserted a comma and wrote on. Likewise, the humorist made excessive use of capitalization; he indiscriminately capitalized nouns, pronouns, adjectives, verbs, prepositions, and conjunctions according to whim. Sometimes he capitalized only the first letter of a word, sometimes the whole word, and on occasions the whole sentence. Although liberal in his use of capitals in his prose, he went to the opposite extreme in omitting apostrophes in contractions and in the possessive case; thus "was not" is usually contracted to "wasnt" or "wasent" and the possessive case is formed by adding "s" or "es" to the nouns concerned.

Although Will did not make any serious attempt to record the speech of a particular region, he did utilize the slang and idiom of the Southwest. The highly colorful speech of the region gave an air of authenticity to his character as a cowboy philosopher. The humorist made considerable use of "aint" as well as other slang expressions such as "lickerty-split," "bust right out," "cuckoo," "buggered up," "a knockout," "hot dog," "nifty," "snooty," "hokum," "cock-eyed," "sitting pretty," "jerky," "mooched up," "rumdum," "geezer," "skypiece," "rag money," "crow hopper," and a host of others. The strong and colorful idiom of the Southwest appeared in such expressions as, "You passed out Poco Pronto," "I got the wrinkles out of my belly," "I had just bull luck," "We stampeded for the Chuck Box," "I had an ol hardtail," "he was hungrier than a She Wolf," and "I lit a shuck for there."

Despite Will's bad grammar, poor punctuation, and slang, few of his readers would have wished him to change his style. It was too well adapted to his stage personality. With a fine disregard for the conventions of grammar, he made no pretense of aiming at a literary style, nor did he consciously attempt to imitate the writing of other humorists. He did, in fact, nothing to improve his literary technique; and how much of his ungrammatical expression was willful, how much was ignorance, and how much was carelessness, no one can say.

III   *Techniques Of Humor*

The real basis of Will's humor lies in his expression of his ideas. Both the form and content of his jokes contribute to his humor, and it is difficult to say which of these elements is more important. Will himself liked to think that exaggeration was the foundation of his humor; but exaggeration is too loose a term to apply to all of his comedy since various degrees of exaggeration produce different reactions. For humorous purposes, it is usually the *too* much, not the much, that is funny. Hence effective exaggeration is based upon the incongruity between what the reader expects and what the humorist provides in an extension of the truth; the incongruity between what the reader thinks as the norm or average as against the humorist's interpretation makes for laughter.

Will's technique was to take the truth and extend it just beyond the realm of possibility, usually not far enough to produce burlesque, but to such an extent that his readers recognized the absurdity. His remarks on the London Naval Conference of 1930 demonstrated this method. As a result of the treaty, he wrote, "Well, we got the treaty signed for the limitation of naval vessels. You hold a conference and decide to sink some vessals that would sink themselves if the conference was postponed for another week. England is to sink three battleships that competed against the Spanish Armada. Japan is raising two that the Russians sunk and will resink them for the treaty and the weeklies. We are building two to sink."[6]

The terms of the treaty announced are true, but the methods of carrying it out are exaggerated beyond the bounds of reason. Had the humorist said that England and Japan were sinking ships of World War I, the statement might be true but not funny. The humor lies in the incongruity between the truth and Will's interpretation of it which is so illogical and inappropriate that it obviously cannot be taken seriously. The incongruity is further heightened by the fact that the humorist pictures England and Japan as reaching into the past to comply with the agreement, which contrasts with the United States which will reach into the future. The idea that the United States will build two ships to sink is just enough of a distortion of the truth to throw the reader off balance and give him the momentary conviction that America has been bested in diplomacy again, which is probably what Will wanted his reader to think. Although the exaggeration of the American role is unpleasant, it is not painful because it is not true; thus it becomes a joke, and the humorist's reputation as a crackerbox philosopher who sees through diplomatic maneuvers is enhanced.

Often Will's remarks contain both perceptual and conceptual qualities which are homogeneous in comic feeling; the perceptual quality acts as a stimulant to the imagination, the creation of an image that looks funny, while the conceptual quality plays a trick upon the mind, a thought process that provokes laughter. Together these qualities provide a broad base for humor — as is evidenced by Mark Twain's book, *Huckleberry Finn*. Most readers find great delight in the visual picture of Huck and Jim, the runaway slave, floating down the river on a raft, as well as much humor in the conversations between the two. Will often used the same technique. When the American diplomats arrived in London for the naval conference, he wrote: "The American delegation arrived this afternoon and went into conference at once at the American Bar and sank a fleet of schooners without warning."[7]

The reader's first reaction is to the perceptual quality of the quip: the picture of sober American diplomats coming to London for a disarmament conference, and immediately going to a bar distorts the importance of their mission. The incongruous picture of dignified diplomats with top hats and frock coats standing around a bar, not usually associated with dignity, is laughter-provoking. But then Will leads his readers on, until their minds abruptly realize that "schooner" is an ambiguous term which may refer to either a naval vessel or a glass of beer; and the obvious meaning is no longer so obvious. Although the humorist has pretended to be heading in a certain direction, he has actually arrived somewhere else; the mind is momentarily tricked; and the consequence is a joke which is rich in flavor.

Although Will's frequent exaggerations and incongruities are genuinely funny, they never reach the colossal proportions of the "tall tales" of the Western humorists; for his objective was to provoke a quiet chuckle rather than boisterous laughter. He once said, "I like jokes where, if you are with a friend and you hear it, it makes you think and nudge your friend and say: 'He's right about that.' " Commenting on military preparedness, he wrote: "If you think preparedness don't give you prestige, look at Japan. We are afraid to look cross-eyed at them for fear of hurting their honor. Before they got a Navy neither them nor us knew they had any Honor. England and Japan would have just as much Honor without a Navy at all, but the Navy helps remind you of it."[8] The incongruity in the suggestion that a powerful navy, a concrete and material perception, is the basis for national honor, an abstract and idealistic conception, is both thought-provoking and amusing. In international affairs, nations pay lip service to the importance of national honor; but they show more respect for a large navy. Thus the apparent relationship is not a logical relationship at all, since abstract and material terms can seldom be equated. The humorist only pretends to believe in the relationship as most of his readers well know.

Much of Will's humor is based upon the element of surprise, as when he inserts a "shocker" in the midst of apparently innocuous remarks. During the depression, he wrote: "Now everybody has got a scheme to relieve unemployment, but there is just one way to do it and thats for everybody to go to work. 'Where?' Why right where you are, look around and you see lots of things to do, weeds to be cut, fences to be fixed, lawns to be mowed, filling stations to be robbed, gangsters to be catered to. . . . Course a man won't get paid for it but he won't get paid for not doing it either."[9] The reader, who is reading and complacently agreeing with the humorist, suddenly comes to "filling stations to be robbed, gangsters to be catered to." The incongruous relationship between the lawful and unlawful methods of work causes a momentary shock before the reader realizes that a practical joke has been played upon his mind, quickly and spontaneously. Will did not really mean for unemployed people to rob filling stations or to cater to gangsters; since these suggestions are so obviously false, foolish, and inappropriate, they cannot be taken seriously, and their failure to mean what they say is part of the joke. There is also humor in the last line, for the humorist provokes the reader into asking, "What will he get for his work?" and then he answers, "Nothing" — a joke on the reader and worker as well.

Sometimes Will used humor as a weapon. He could be ironic, satiric, sardonic, or caustic on issues about which he felt real concern. In an ironic vein, the humorist, like Socrates, often pretended ignorance himself in order to expose the foolishness and hypocrisy of others. "I am just an ignorant feller, without any education" he would say, and then proceed to puncture the pretenses of learned authorities. When President Harding and the Steel Trust were discussing the demands of labor for a shorter working day, Rogers wrote:

Well, I see by this morning's papers that our old friend, Mr. Gary of the Steel trust, after much letter writing and persuasion from President Harding, has promised the President that he would do away with the 12 hour a day work in the steel mills (just as soon as it could be arranged) . . . Mr. Gary says that it will take time. You see a man who has been working for years for 13 or 14 hours a day, and you cut him down to 8 and you have a physical wreck on your hands. You take a person who is used to the cool air of the steel furnace for half the 24 hours of each day and bring him into the stuffy atmosphere outdoors, or at home, and he cant stand it.[10]

Here the seemingly humble and ignorant Will is exposing the pretension of Mr. Gary, who, as the leader of the Steel Trust, presumably is an authority on the labor problem. Mr. Gary's remark on "time" probably relates to the problem of adjusting equipment to meet production demands, but the humorist chooses to interpret it as referring only to the laborer. Consequently, Rogers makes fun of Mr. Gary's remark by understating his own position to the point of absurdity. Again there is incongruity between the "cool air" of the "steel furnace" and the "stuffy atmosphere outdoors." Although the subject is not funny, the remarks are humorous because the reader knows that Will meant exactly the opposite of what he said. The statement became strong irony because the humorist took nothing at all and made it mean a great deal.

Another of Will's methods of using humor as a weapon was to play the role of the "fool" character who is unable to understand the obvious. In this role, the humorist pretends to be naive and unsuspecting of the motives of people who make statements that are obviously untrue. During Prohibition, temperance leaders tried to get the United States government to exert pressure on the Mexican government to close down the border cities of Tia Juana and Mexicali by alleging that these cities were a corrupting influence on American tourists. Will wrote:

Americans don't want to drink and gamble. They just go over there to see the mountains and these scheming Mexicans grab 'em and make 'em drink, and make 'em make bets, and make 'em watch the race Horses run for money. It seems that Americans don't know these places are over there at all, and when they get there these Mexicans spring on 'em and they have to drink or the Mexicans will kill 'em. All in the world we have to do to keep our Citizens pure and good like they have been all this time is not allow them over the line. If we have to admit that we were raising people that don't know enough to take proper care of themselves, we will have to do it by another Amendment as follows: Americans are not allowed anywhere where they will be subject to evil influences.[11]

The obvious target of Will's humorous attack is the sanctimonious attempt on the part of the prohibitionists to legislate the morality of another country. He pretends indignation at the thought of "pure" Americans on a sight-seeing tour being forced into "sin" by scheming Mexicans. Since his readers knew well enough why Americans went to Tia Juana and Mexicali, Will's indignation is not only naive but inappropriate since the reality of the situation is the exact opposite of what has been described. The "fool's" simple solution to keep Americans "good" and "pure" by passing a law to prevent them from being exposed to "evil influences" is an attack upon the mistaken belief of the prohibitionists that personal morality can be legislated. The overexaggeration and oversimplification of the "fool" character simply reminds the reader of the hypocrisy and foolishness of the temperance movement.

Because Will Rogers was so intimately connected with the political scene, he not infrequently used his humor, as did Mr. Dooley, to point to some deficiency in the political or social situation. In fact, political satire in America during the 1920's and 1930's was virtually the monopoly of Will Rogers. This form of humor has always been the weapon of the common man; and, although the cowboy humorist never brandished it as heavily as Finley Peter Dunne, he used it effectively in his attacks upon issues important to him. However, since Rogers had the role of satirist thrust upon him, his comments are only rarely as penetrating as Mr. Dooley's. He was at his best when he felt strongly about some action. On the question of Philippine independence, he wrote: "You refuse to give the Philippines their independence. I am with you. Why should the Philippines have more than we do?"[12]

There is no question about Will's real feeling about Philippine independence. What he is doing is simply tearing away the veil of American smugness and self-satisfaction which had developed through paying lip service to the idea of freedom while denying it to the Filipinos for political and economic reasons. His remark is humorous because it is an attack upon a fundamental American belief which is made ridiculous in the spirit of pure fun.

In the same manner, Will struck at government inefficiency during the depression.

Here is what George Washington missed by not living to his 199th birthday. He would have seen our great political system of "equal rights to all and the privileges to none" working so smoothly that 7,000,000 are without a chance to earn their living; he would have seen 'em handing out rations in peace times — that would have reminded him of Valley Forge. In fact we have reversed the old system; we all get fat in war time and thin during peace. I bet after seeing us he would sue us for calling him "father."[13]

Here the object of attack is the government. Literally, the humorist is saying that there is something wrong with a government that permits so high a number of its citizens to be unemployed. But the manner of expression is frivolous. The suggestion that Washington "missed" something by not living 199 years is smile-provoking because the idea is absurd. It borders on the ludicrous — just as Mark Twain's absurdity did in feigning grief over the death of Adam, his ancestor, who did not live to see him. But in Will's remark, the element of satire lies in the obvious "untruth" that the political system is working so smoothly as to produce undesirable results. Since unemployment is not the proper aim of government, the reader must wryly acknowledge the truth: the government is not functioning properly. What the humorist has said and what he has meant are two different things. He has struck at the government without taking it seriously; in so doing, he has exposed a weakness.

Sometimes Will's remarks are written in a spirit of pure fun. Once, when in a playful mood, he wrote a parody of Shakespeare which approaches burlesque in its extreme exaggeration:

To inflate or not to inflate, that is the Democratic question. Whether it is nobler in mind to suffer the slings and arrows of southern politicians, or to take up inflation against a sea of economists and by opposing end them. To expand, to inflate, to inflate, perchance to dream. Aye, there's the rub. For in that sleep of inflation, what dreams may come, puzzle the will and make us doubt whether to bear these ills we have, than fly to others we know not of.[14]

To his readers who were familiar with *Hamlet*, the incongruity of the comparison of a group of Democrat politicians with Hamlet the Dane was ludicrous. Moreover, there is a strong quality of burlesque in the suggestion that the indecision of Hamlet was comparable to the problems of a political party whose motives, as Will and his readers well knew, were prompted by considerations which Shakespeare never dreamed of. The playful wit of the humorous substitutions, slings and arrows of southern politicians, and "sea of economists" provided a jocular element which had real meaning in the early days of the New Deal and made for delightful fooling.

Another characteristic of Will's humor was his use of the "punch line" or "snapper" at the end of his columns. Almost invariably the final sentence summarizes the essence of his thought and expresses it in a thought-provoking manner. For example, the humorist wrote a column concerning the retirement of General John J. Pershing from the United States Army:

80 thousand people paid 800 thousand dollars to see twelve rounds of wrestling between Wills and Firpo (for the heavyweight boxing championship of the world). On the same day those alleged Fighters received 150 thousand Dollars cash for 36 minutes embracing why we released on half salary General Pershing who had spent 42 years fighting for his Country. During 42 years his whole total Salary paid to him by (what is sometimes humorously referred to as a liberal Government) never amount to what these men received in 36 minutes. . . . So if you are thinking of taking up fighting as a career why be sure and FIGHT FOR YOURSELF INSTEAD OF FOR YOUR COUNTRY.[15]

The "punch line" not only serves to summarize the idea but is couched in such terms as to make it easy to remember. Writing about the amount of income tax paid by the wealthy families of America Will said, "Don't feel discouraged if a lot of our well known men were not as wealthy according to their Tax as you thought they ought to be. They are just as rich as you thought. This publication of amounts had nothing to with their wealth. It was only a test of their honesty, and gives you practically no idea of their wealth at all."[16] Such lines also enhanced the humorist's reputation as a crackerbox philosopher who could sum up a complicated problem in a few short words.

IV *Cacography and Puns*

In the development of his humorous style, Will Rogers used many of the verbal devices made popular by American humorists in the nineteenth century; these include cacography, puns, and comic metaphors. Although cacography does not seem hilariously funny to the reader of today, Will's generation still found humor in the device so successfully exploited by Artemus Ward, Josh Billings, and Abe Martin. One must consider the history of English spelling to understand why nineteenth-century Americans found misspelling so highly amusing. During that century, most Americans prided themselves upon their ability to read and write; and skill in spelling was considered proof of literacy. Since spelling was so highly regarded, misspelling constituted a kind of disrespect for authority.

Cacography in Will was never an art. In fact it is difficult, as has been observed, to tell where he deliberately misspelled either to maintain a pretense of ignorance or to be humorous; where he misspelled through carelessness or ignorance with no humor intended. Yet he recognized the value of word distortion in producing a comic effect, and there are many examples of what might properly be termed cacography in his work. A partial list includes: "vulumes" (volumes), "spaecial" (special), "superfolous" (superfluous), "komical" (comical), "tee bone" (T bone), "neglije" (negligee), "poet lariat" (poet laureate), "nise" (nice), "centanial" (centennial), "doe" (dough), "ballotts" (ballots), "shouffer" (chauffeur), "consome" (consomme), "bee" (be), "fraternoty" (fraternity), "visay" (visa), "Rottary" (Rotary), "passafist" (pacifist), "gallowses" (galluses), "injun" (Indian), "staid" (stayed), "leery" (leary), and "nerer" (nearer).

Some of these distortions are more than simple misspellings. A few are obvious puns as in "poet lariat," "bee," and "doe." In some of the words, the peculiar spelling creates a meaning which is incongruous to the original meaning; the spelling of "passafist," for pacifist, for example, carries a negative impression of the real word. And "frater*noty*" suggests that fraternities are "not frater" or not brothers.

Sometimes Will's spelling seems to indicate that he is trying to record the idiom of the Southwest in his writing; thus many of his apparently misspelled words are not words at all but merely his attempt to reproduce the sound of oral English. The humorist normally uses "er" and "a" to represent the slurring together of two words: "Kinder" (kind of), "orter" (ought to), "sorter" (sort of), "woulda" (would have), and "coulda" (could have). Other peculiar locutions include the use of "a" as a prefix for participles as "aliving," "acoming," and "atrying"; the use of the suffix "t" for "ed" as in "stopt," "wisht," and "lookt"; and the omission of the apostrophe in contractions such as "cant," "dont," "wont," and "dident."

Among the lighter veins of humor, Will had a fondness for puns. Although he was not a punster in the extreme sense, he enjoyed playing with words when the opportunity presented itself. Most of his word play resulted in rather obvious puns where the shift of meaning seems frivolous rather than witty. For example, he once gave a radio speech in imitation of Calvin Coolidge: "I am proud to report that the condition of the country as a whole is prosperous. I dont mean that the whole country is prosperous, but that as a hole it is prosperous. That is, it is prosperous for a hole. There is not a whole lot of doubt about that."[17] The length of the expression served as assurance that none of his listeners would miss the obvious shift in the word "whole." There is no real meaning involved in the change from "whole" (in general) to 'whole" (total) thence to "hole" (excavation); the ambiguous nature of the word as it is pronounced, whether as an adjective or as a noun, whether abstract or concrete, is the basis for the pun.

Some of his puns, however, are packed with meaning. Writing of the relationship between the United States and Mexico, he said that "The difference in our exchange of people with Mexico is; they send workmen here to work, while we send Americans there to 'work' Mexico." Commenting on a New Deal Congress, he wrote, "Mentally the boys are befuddled, but they are in the 'pink.' (That's what the fellows with the dough are afraid of, there is too many of 'em in the 'pink.')." The word shift in the first quip from "work" (to labor) to the slang "work" (to trick), and in the second joke from "pink" (good physical condition) to "pink" (a Communist sympathizer) is witty because, in the word play, the context takes on a new and plausible meaning.

Max Eastman believed that Will's best pun was one on Pancho Villa: "I see by the headlines that Villa excapes Net and Flees. We will never catch him then. Any Mexican that can escape Fleas is beyond catching." On a wager with Will, Eastman distinguished ten points in which this joke excelled the common pun: first, the subject matter is interesting; second, the plausibility is perfect; third, we are encouraged to keep moving forward; fourth, the collapse of the verbal vehicle is unforeseen; fifth, the understanding of the shift from a verb to a noun is comprehensive; sixth, we easily recover our balance; seventh, the new line of thought leads to a superior attitude since fleas are more common in Mexico than in America; eighth, the second idea makes sense because we cannot catch Villa anyway; ninth, there is incongruity in a man escaping a military net as against a man escaping fleas; and, tenth, a man escaping fleas is funny anyway.[18]

Will was also partial to the comic metaphor or simile. Reared in the Southwest, he had a habit of expressing himself in pungent figures of speech which reflected his background. His cowboy heritage combined with his interest in politics to create some incongruous metaphors which were both colorful and humorous. In speaking of a horseshoe tournament in Florida, he wrote, "The Champion Mule Slipper Slingers of the world are at St. Petersburg . . . They can take a pair of second hand Horses low quarters and hang 'em on a peg more times than a dry Congressman can reach for his hip pocket." At a bull fight in Mexico, he wrote, "That bull emptied the ring like a speech on the tarriff will the Senate Gallery." Americans, he observed, are like Ford cars — "They all have the same parts, the same upholstery and make exactly the same noises." Writing on party politics, he said "A Guy raised in a straight jacket is a Corkscrew compared to a thick headed Party Politician." Hearing of a revolution in South America, he wrote, "A revolution is just like one cocktail, it just gets you organized for the next." After a naval conference, he said, "To reduce your navy is exactly like a man who is not doing so well financially cancelling all his life insurance, figuring its a dead loss because he hasent died yet."

V Philosophy of Humor

The pattern of Will's technique, both in form and expression, reflected his personal philosophy of humor. Early in his career as a vaudeville comedian, the humorist developed a formula for his jokes from which he seldom deviated. After he became successful, he was asked many times about his views on humor; and he always gave the same answer: he tried to make his jokes on up-to-date subjects; he preferred to keep his quips short; and he liked to base his remarks on some element of the truth.[19]

For the topical humor which Will wrote, his concept of the importance of timeliness seems essential. Most humorists recognize that there are no new jokes, only old ones recast into new surroundings; consequently, Rogers seems to have learned early that old humorous material could be made effective by relating it to current topics of public interest. When he said over and over that his humor always related to the "now," he did not mean, however, that his comedy *depended* on timeliness for its effect since the form of his material is often funny in itself; but, because most of his humor was related to topical events which *at the time* were of great public interest, the impact of his jokes was reinforced. Will had such a high regard for timeliness that Max Eastman said of him, "he had a keener sense of the kinship between humor and the present moment than any other humorist I know."[20]

In the tradition of Franklin, Billings, and other nineteenth-century humorists, Will practiced terseness as an element of his humor. Few of his jokes ran over five or six lines, and his weekly column was a series of short jokes loosely connected together. The humorist once said, "Being brief somehow gives the impression of intelligence, and folks do admire intelligence. Brevity and clarity show that you have done some thinking, and that you know what you are talking about."[21] Thus he liked to create sharp, terse phrases which could be easily remembered and which contained a great deal of common sense. Summarizing the European situation in 1934, he wrote, "Chili is selling nitrates, Europe is fertilizing again." Or, speaking of peace conferences: "I have a scheme for stopping war. It's this — no nation is allowed to enter a war till they have paid for the last one." Utterances like these made his followers chuckle, agree with him, and repeat his words to their friends.

The fundamental quality, however, of Will's humor — and the one he thought most important — was truth. He liked to think that all of his jokes were rooted deep in the subsoil of reality. Explaining his technique, he said, "I use only one set method in my little gags, and exaggerate it, but what you say must be based upon the truth."[22] Since most of his material was taken from the daily papers, his humor was based upon the truth, as he saw it and he believed it to be. For example, in referring to American diplomacy, he wrote, "Our Foreign Dealings are an Open Book — usually a Check Book." The humor of this joke is as much in the form as in the content. The mental incongruity which develops as the mind leaps from "Open Book" (figurative) to "Check Book" (literal) becomes a seeming congruity as the mind is directed back to "Open Book," which now becomes a literal expression meaning "open to make payments." Thus the humorist forces the mind into a crazy pattern to reach his meaning. But the content reinforces the humor, since people who read the joke and believe it to be true will find it more humorous than those who do not think it true. In other words, only those who agree with the statement will think of the humorist as a crackerbox philosopher; those who find the incongruity amusing, but the content not true, may think of the humorist as perhaps ignorant or uninformed.

When Will spoke of his jokes as being based on the truth, he did not mean factual truth but truth as he thought of it. Much of his reputation as a crackerbox philosopher rested on the fact that a majority of his readers usually agreed with him; they felt that most of what he said was true and more sensible than other pronouncements on the same subject.

By and large, the humor of Will Rogers reflected the same techniques employed by the old-time American humorists. As both a lecturer and a writer, he used the same expressions, the same devices, and the same manners as his predecessors. He used them so successfully that not a few of his readers thought of him as the greatest humorist the country had produced, for he embodied to many Americans a type of crackerbox philosopher which seemed more representative of the country than any humorist before him.

CHAPTER 6

Will Rogers and the
Crackerbox Tradition

❝ A MERICANS have had a long tradition of philosophers in homespun," wrote Henry Seidel Canby in 1935. "Homespun in mind they have all been, which means that, whatever the source of their wisdom, its form and expression was distinctly local to this continent, and many of them have been homely also in speech, self-made in knowledge, and blatantly provincial."[1] This type of expression characterizes a genre of humor based on an American belief in common sense, particularly such common sense as is expressed by an unlettered philosopher who becomes a symbol or personification of the folk. Since this crackerbox philosopher reflects the viewpoint of the common people, his homely wisdom and shrewd observations on the life about him become both socially and politically significant to the Americans of his epoch.

This homely wisdom, or "horse sense," as it is often called, is native to the American scene. To most Americans, "horse sense" stands for good, sound, practical common sense:

A man blessed with mother-wit in this meaning of the words, Americans think, is lucky in that he can handle whatever problems he has to face — deal with them properly. He does not have to look into a book to find the answers, does not have to ask anybody on earth what to do. He can solve his own problems because he was born with a long head on him, he has "been around," and has learned everything he can from experience. When he gets into a new situation, he whittles his problem down to its essentials, sees how it compares with situations in his past and how it differs from them, and then he thinks out what he should do — figures out the right answer.[2]

A curious consistency about the appearance of this homely type occurs in American literature which suggests that the crackerbox philosopher has had a peculiar attraction to the American mind. Through the years, Benjamin Franklin, Jack Downing, Hosea

Biglow, Artemus Ward, Petroleum V. Nasby, Bill Nye, Josh Billings, Mark Twain, and Martin Dooley have been successive representations of the horse-sense philosopher; and the last clear example of the type is Will Rogers. The relationship of Will to the long line of crackerbox humorists is apparent in both his form and expression, for he utilized many of the established techniques of the old-time American humorists. Yet in many ways he was unique: his background as a cowboy and vaudeville performer, the modernity of the age in which he lived, and the many mediums through which he reached his audiences caused him to deviate from the established patterns of earlier humor. Yet, despite these differences, his mind operated in much the same fashion as the earlier horse-sense humorists, and he earned most of his laughs in the same old ways.[3]

In the development of the crackerbox philosopher as a type in American humor, there were frequent differences in the characters created by the humorists; but the basic common-sense formula remained constant. In Benjamin Franklin's *Dogood Papers* (1722), Widow Silence Dogood emerged as an unlettered but canny observer of New England affairs. With her scorn for theoretical knowledge, such as that learned in college, and her inelegant colloquial phrasing, the Widow Dogood was Franklin's first horse-sense character. In 1732, Franklin spoke to his countrymen through the guise of Richard Saunders, whose commonplace wisdom, resulting from his personal experience, reflected Franklin's own belief in practical morality. A forerunner of the Yankee character, Richard Saunders, the ostensible author of the *Almanac,* was a man of little formal learning but of much practical down-to-earth experience. His shrewd observations about how to succeed in life were generally based on materialistic concerns and moral doctrines. So well did he preach his lessons of thrift, frugality, and godliness that, with the publication in 1757 of *The Way to Wealth,* a collection of his aphorisms, his reputation was firmly established as a man of gumption and uncommon common sense. Poor Richard's sayings became a part of the American experience.

The humor of Will Rogers often reflected the same homely sagacity, for he too based his moral philosophy on practical considerations rather than on idealistic principles; and, like Franklin's Richard Saunders, Will expressed his common-sense pronouncements in an unlettered style. Just as Richard could project an idea in a pithy aphorism such as "Beware of small expenses. A small leak can sink a great ship" or "By diligence and patience, the mouse bit in two the cable," so Will could summarize a whole column in a short "snapper" line as when he wrote about a reparations conference to which the United States was not invited that "you can't have a picnic lunch unless the party carrying the basket comes," or when he remarked about partisan politicians, "Party politics will never be changed because you cant change human nature. You cant broaden a man's vision if he wasent born with one."

Both Franklin and Will made a habit of offering advice to the American people. In the *Almanac,* Franklin through his mouthpiece, Poor Richard, was not merely concerned about the way in which farmers planted and reaped their crops but about rearing children, supervising maids and servants, and choosing a wife. "A wife," said Poor Richard, "can be a help or hindrance so Keep your eyes wide open before marriage; half shut afterwards." In a like manner, Will prescribed remedies for American economic ills during the depression: "What this country needs is more working men and fewer politicians."

Aside from his similarity to Franklin, Will also had a distinct affinity for the wit of the Yankee crackerbox philosopher. The Yankee type in American humor apparently began during the Revolution as a caricature of the rustic rebel, and he appeared as a national figure for the first time in 1787 as Jonathan in Royall Tyler's comedy, *The Contrast.* Thereafter, a whole series of plays initiated this Yankee characterization. At the same time, the almanacs, periodical essays, and novels used the type, so that, by the turn of the century, he had become a stock figure of American literature. The early Jonathan, however, was more a clown than a wit; he appeared in comedy roles, and only occasionally displayed native shrewdness. Finally, Seba Smith, editor of the *Portland Courier,* created a Yankee who was something more than the conventional stage comedian.

In 1830, Smith created Jack Downing, the first realistic, unlettered philosopher in American literature whose humor was based primarily upon folk material. During the administration of Andrew Jackson, Downing's audacious comments about national politics and political figures had a strong appeal to the native irreverence and common sense of his readers. Written in Yankee dialect with its characteristic idiom and spelling, the Downing letters were breezily impudent in describing the activities of the Jackson administration and the national legislature. The same vein of humor is found in Will Rogers' columns in his comments about the national political scene.

In the Downing letters, Jack described his visits with Old Andy (Andrew Jackson) and Little Van (Martin Van Buren) who received him in their shirt sleeves and talked freely with him about affairs of national importance. As Downing told it, he was a member of the Kitchen Cabinet to whom the President turned for advice, and a trusted confidant to whom Jackson once said, "Major Downing, you are the boy for me; I don't know how I should get along in this world if it wasn't for you." In the same manner, Will told his readers about his conversations with the great men of public affairs — Presidents, Congressmen, business leaders, diplomats, and public heroes. Like Jack, he presented such individuals as quite ordinary people who were glad to exchange the time of day and to explain the intricacies of their business to an ignorant cowboy. Besides describing his visits to the White House and his conversations with Presidents Coolidge and Roosevelt, he described a meeting with the Prince of Wales where "we just talked like a couple of old Hill Billies," and his interview with Mussolini where "I felt as much at home with him as I could with Dinty Moore on 46th St." And, like Downing, who made few scurrilous attacks upon political leaders directly, Will turned most of his satiric slants at party politicians in general, seldom singling out any individual in particular for criticism.

Will also used some of the devices of that best-known of all Yankee crackerbox philosophers, Hosea Biglow, created in 1816 by James Russell Lowell. Speaking in an authentic rustic dialect, for Lowell was a master of rural New England speech, Hosea employed his native gumption and wit to expose the foolishness and hypocrisy displayed during the Mexican and Civil wars. Just as Hosea used Yankee turns of phrases and made homely allusions to New England, so did Will Rogers cling to the colorful idiom of the Southwest and make constant references to his hometown of Claremore, and to his background as a cowboy. Thus Hosea scorns the recruiting sergeant's technique, for "Tain't a knowin kind o' cattle that is ketched with mouldy corn"; and he admires Governor Briggs because "He stays to his home an' looks arter his folks; He draws his furror as straight oz he can, An' into nobody's tater-patch pokes." In the same way, Will is scornful of the Tiber River which "couldn't be a tributary to the Grand, Canadian, or Verdigris back home"; and he admires Paris because it is "the Claremore, Oklahoma, of France."

By 1850, the crackerbox philosopher had become a standard type in American humor. Chief among the fun-makers of the Civil War and Reconstruction era were the itinerant showman, Artemus Ward, created by Charles Farrar Browne in 1858, and the hypocritical Copperhead, Petroleum V. Nasby, created by David Ross Locke in 1861. Both Ward and Nasby cracked jokes which were sometimes inane and sometimes vulgar, but their witticisms interpreted human nature as they saw it and pointed cogently to the imperfections of the current social order. During the same period, Josh Billings, the characterization of Henry Wheeler Shaw in 1860, published his essays and aphorisms, expressing the same homely wit and common-sense philosophy.

The relationship of Will Rogers to these literary comedians is apparent in his form and expression. Like Ward, Nasby, and Billings, he utilized, as has already been noted, cacography, poor grammar, illogical punctuation, homely metaphors, and regional idioms. Like them, he gave the impression of illiteracy and ignorance, thus leading his readers to believe he had little respect for book learning. Just as Ward ridiculed the Shakers and the Mormons, so did Will poke fun at the Ku Klux Klan and the fundamentalists. As much as Nasby, Will had a fondness for stringing together all sorts of incongruous objects and a liking for puns. The pithy, aphoristic expressions of Billings were echoed in the "snapper" lines of Will's columns.

Will also had much in common with Mark Twain, who began writing humor as early as 1865. Twain's early humor, written in the West, employed many of the devices used by Ward and Nasby in the East. But, as Walter Blair emphasizes, Mark, as he became more famous, discarded the dialect and twisted grammar of the literary comedians, and his humor turned on the incongruities developed by contrasting the fool way of thinking and talking with the wise way of seeing and expressing things.[4]

Mark Twain, of course, never lost his delight in puns, comic metaphor, and anti-climactic sentences; but, as a crackerbox philosopher, he liked to show the contrast between native wit and book learning, instinctive ways of thinking and learned ways of reasoning. Like the elder humorist, Will Rogers preferred to base his humor on incongruities developed by exaggeration. As provincial as Twain when it came to judging things European in comparison with

American institutions, Will seemed bored and unimpressed with the cultural and historical splendors which Europe offered, preferring instead the material advantages and the practical values of his own country. The remarks of the cowboy humorist about the great Italian artists, Michelangelo and Leonardo da Vinci, are amazingly similar to Mark's comments in *Innocents Abroad*. Both Twain and Rogers came from the West; and, since the stamp of the frontier was upon them, they were suspicious of intellectuals, but supremely confident of the value of their own practical experience.

In the later part of the nineteenth century, Finley Peter Dunne, a newspaper man in Chicago, broke slightly with the crackerbox tradition. He took the unlettered philosopher from the village and placed him in the city. Through the guise of a Chicago saloon keeper, Martin Dooley, Dunne lambasted and lampooned the social, economic, and political evils of his era. Despite his lack of book learning, Mr. Dooley knew human nature; and his common-sense remarks about the affairs of his day were strikingly sound.

Many of the elements of Mr. Dooley's humor are found in that of Will Rogers. Like Mr. Dooley, Rogers questioned the sincerity of politicians, the honesty of financiers, the value of patriotic speeches, and the wisdom of expansionist policies; and, like the Irish saloon keeper, he was indignant over any betrayal of public trust. Just as Dooley treated famous and wealthy personages as no better than his own neighbors, so did Will casually refer to prominent men of affairs as if they were ordinary citizens. Dooley spoke familiarly of Cousin George (Dewey), Mack (McKinley), and Teddy (Roosevelt); Will made reference to Al (Smith), Cal (Coolidge), and John D. (Rockefeller).

From Ben Franklin to Will Rogers, then, the line of crackerbox philosophers in American humor was unbroken. Nevertheless, the relationship of Will to the tradition only partially explains his humor. Of equal importance are the ways in which he differed from his literary predecessors. With the possible exception of Mark Twain, no American humorist ever enjoyed as great a popularity as Will, or had a stronger impact upon his fellow Americans. Perhaps his popularity can be explained by examining the characteristics of the Oklahoman which distinguished him from his literary ancestors, and the distinctions between his humor and theirs.

One important difference between Will Rogers and the humorists before him was that his stage personality was entirely natural for

him. In stepping from private life into the public eye, the humorist
affected a pose of ignorance and illiteracy; but, otherwise, everything
about him — his appearance, his clothing, his speech, his gestures —
bespoke his background and environment. If he appeared before his
audiences as a cowboy philosopher, it was because he had been a
cowboy, reared in Indian Territory. If his speech and writing displayed faulty pronunciation and poor grammar, it was because he actually had had little formal education. If he appeared sagacious and
understanding, it was because he had learned through experience to
apply common-sense remedies to his problems.

Each of the humorists before Will had been one person in private
life and another in his character as a horse-sense humorist. Few people confused James Russell Lowell, the erudite Bostonian, with
Hosea Biglow, or thought of Charles Farrar Browne, editor of the
Cleveland *Plain Dealer,* as being like the itinerant showman,
Artemus Ward, or accepted Finley Peter Dunne as the Chicago
saloon keeper, Martin Dooley. The characters themselves were
amusing, witty, and wise; but they were recognized as literary
creations who spoke for their particular creators; they were not
creatures of flesh and blood. With Will Rogers, the general public
apparently made no such distinction; it judged him as one and the
same in his person and in his character as a humorist.

On the lecture platform, Will's appearance served to confirm his
naturalness. To audiences who had read his columns and heard his
radio broadcasts, he looked as a cowboy philosopher should.
Although he affected a look of surprised innocence at the response to
his humor, just as Mark Twain did, Will shunned most of the
affected mannerisms of dress and gesture employed by Artemus
Ward, Bill Nye, and Josh Billings who deliberately assumed the
manner and toggery of the clown.

In fact, many of these professional humorists were close to being
the modern equivalent of the old court jesters: creatures of motley
who were admitted to have some sense about them, they had to
appear under a disguise if they wished to be taken seriously. Thus
Henry Wheeler Shaw, in his stage role of Josh Billings, assumed a
melancholy solemnity of demeanor which enhanced the incongruity
of his humorous pronouncements; and Bill Nye, a lanky, bald-
headed man in formal attire, affected the absurd dignity and earnest
manner of a man totally unconscious of the humor of his remarks.
By contrast, Will Rogers' infectious grin and informal manner

created a sense of intimacy between him and his audience that was almost irresistible.

Will's language and literary expression were in keeping with his public personality; his poor grammar, misspellings, and illogical sentence constructions were not inappropriate for a cowboy philosopher. The racy, colloquial, slanglike idiom of the Southwest was familiar to him; and he never felt either embarrassed or apologetic about ungrammatical structure. He wrote and spoke as he did because he felt that he could communicate his ideas more directly in the pungent language to which he was accustomed. By contrast, the ungrammatical expressions of most of the crackerbox philosophers, except James Russell Lowell, seem contrived and artificial. The misshapen words and sentences of Josh Billings, for example, were quite unlike the normal speech of Henry Wheeler Shaw, a former Hamilton College student, who had by turns been a farmer, a coal operator, a captain, and proprietor of a steamboat. He had written humorous pieces for several years without any great success until 1860 when he turned to cacography and queer grammar in *An Essa on the Muel bi Josh Billings*. Success crowned his effort, and from that time on, Shaw never deviated from his successful formula of warping grammar and spelling out of its normal form. Likewise Browne, Locke, and Nye consciously twisted the language of their characters for the purpose of humor. There is no doubt that these devices were successful, but the contrived nature of the expression is easily recognized.

On the other hand, Mark Twain's most interesting contribution to the humor of horsesense was in *Tom Sawyer* and *Huckleberry Finn,* and in these books much of the charm and humor lies in the natural quality of the boys' speech; the slang and colloquialisms employed by both Tom and Huck give an air of authenticity to their discourse. This same realistic manner of expression helped to enhance Will's reputation as a cowboy philosopher, for his language was not appreciably different from that of others in the Southwest.

Will's humor is also set apart from that of his predecessors by the quantity and quality of his writing. Few American humorists have written so much and so humorously with so little literary training. His literary apprenticeship consisted of ten years of experience in conceiving short jokes to be delivered during his rope twirling act while he was in vaudeville. Yet without any literary training, or a pretense of style, he wrote sustained humor for publication for six-

teen years; and at no time during that period was there any evidence
that the public was tiring of his jests.

By contrast, most of his forerunners had considerable literary experience before they turned to humor: Seba Smith, Charles Farrar
Browne, David Ross Locke, Finley Peter Dunne, Samuel Clemens,
and Edgar W. Nye were competent journalists and practiced writers.
These humorists were professional writers in the strictest sense, but
Will was more properly a professional entertainer for whom writing
was only one medium of expression for his art. Yet he wrote four independent books, a weekly column syndicated for thirteen years, a
daily column for eight years, and many articles for periodicals. In
sheer bulk, he is exceeded only by Mark Twain; and much of the
elder humorist's literary work must be classified outside the field of
humor.

Although Will wrote sustained humor for over sixteen years,
paradoxically enough he seemed incapable of creating long pieces of
humorous writing. The quality of his humor was at its best in his
short, daily column which expressed clearly, wittily, and concisely
what millions of his readers had been thinking vaguely. His longer
columns show a lack of unity and structure when compared to the essays and books of Bill Nye, Mark Twain, and Martin Dooley. All of
these humorists were capable of developing a theme into an in-
tegrated expression in which the humor of the part was always subor-
dinated to the humor of the whole. Fredrick Van de Water, literary
critic of the *New York Herald Tribune,* noted this difference in com-
paring Will with Mark Twain: "In sustained work, Will Rogers is infinitely the inferior of Clemens. He is by nature a paragrapher,
speaking his comments upon the foolishness of mortals instead of
writing it. . . . Page by page there can be no comparison between
Rogers and Twain. But paragraph by paragraph will not always
bring the elder humorist the victory. There is no one, we think, who
can say so much in so few words as Will Rogers."[5] The same quality
in Will's writing has also been noted by others: Will Rogers wrote
good paragraphs but did not have that capability of writing a good
book.

Perhaps Rogers' tendency toward short, pungent expressions was
the result of his commitment to write a daily and weekly column in a
humorous vein. Few other American humorists ever placed such a
strain upon their wit. Mark Twain, for example, once refused a
handsome offer for a weekly column of humor because he felt that

such a schedule would exhaust his capacity for fun-making. Mr. Dooley's columns appeared on a weekly basis; but Elmer Ellis, author of *Mr. Dooley's America,* wrote that Finley Peter Dunne struggled at times to prepare his weekly article: "Sometimes he refused, and the space had to be filled with a substitute, but more often he let it go until near press time, and then he would produce it under pressure with a copy boy carrying a few sentences at a time to the typesetter."[6] Will Rogers, too, felt the strain of his commitment and tried to drop his weekly article; but he was persuaded by the McNaught syndicate to continue it.

Another distinction between Will Rogers and other crackerbox philosophers was his lack of political partisanship and crusading spirit. Because he thought of himself as an entertainer rather than a reformer, his observations of human frailities seldom aroused in him the same indignation which burned in the breasts of other more passionate reformers such as Lowell, Twain, and Dunne. During the Mexican War and the Civil War, Lowell vigorously championed the Abolitionist movement, creating Hosea Biglow and Birdofredum Sawin to unmask the sham and hypocrisy of the slavery expansionists, the war mongers, and the Southern politicians; Twain waxed bitter and struck savagely at injustice, against aristocracy, and toward all forms of organized tyranny; and Dooley turned his wit against all demagoguery, and against the American feeling of national and racial superiority.

Will, too, struck at ideas and issues which he thought contrary to public good; but he was so good-natured with his scorn and criticism that few of those whom he attacked harbored any grudge against him. As to his impartiality, it was not due to indifference, nor calculation, nor any sense of superiority; he was more interested in people than in issues; and he preferred to play no favorites. His satire probably suffered because of the mediums through which he worked and the changing circumstances of the times. Furthermore, as Walter Blair pointed out, Will never felt the towering anger which Mark Twain turned against everything he disliked. Twain's bitterness and anger which saturated his later work, sometimes marred his humor; but Will Rogers had no hate, hence his remarks, though sometimes candid and caustic about items which involved him deeply, never seriously offended those under attack.[7]

Another unique quality which elevated Will to the top rank of crackerbox philosophers was his role as "opinion maker" for the

American mind. To a certain extent, all horse-sense characters since Ben Franklin have affected the American thought of their own generation. But Will seems to have possessed an amazing faculty for expressing what the average man believed or wanted to hear, and his daily messages became an important factor in molding public opinion. Unquestionably the Downing letters, the Biglow Papers, and the war-time humor of Nasby and Arp were influential in shaping the public mind; but their scope was considerably narrower. Between 1898 and 1910, Mr. Dooley had a potent effect on the American mind; presidents and congressmen were particularly sensitive to his exposures of hollowness and sham, but he lacked the mediums through which Will reached such a large number of people.

Through the mediums of radio and syndicated columns, Will's thoughts were circulated throughout the United States and Europe. Even in England the cowboy humorist was recognized. S.S. Ratcliffe, a London commentator, wrote, "His, indeed, was almost the only American voice which carried over the whole country and was listened to by everyone . . . when, in March last, the Senate came to a decisive vote on America's entry [the World Court] Will Rogers was allied with the Hearst Press against the Court. In that decision, the philosopher exercised a much wider power than the radio-priest, Father Coughlin, to whom the victory of the die-hards was chiefly attributed at that time."[8] His influence was such that Walter Lippmann, the distinguished commentator, felt called upon to rebuke Will publicly for misquoting a campaign promise made by President Hoover. This public reprimand indicated that Lippmann gave Will a place among the opinion makers whose influence Lippmann himself held it vital to counteract because it was so powerful.

Indeed, the faith which the common people had in Will was little short of phenomenal. He became firmly entrenched in the minds of his countrymen as the apotheosis of the average man, and millions of Americans seem to have had an extraordinary trust and belief in him. Because he appeared sagacious but not pretentious, experienced but not sophisticated, his observations on the state of the nation and on international affairs were accepted almost without question by his admirers. His ideas were accepted, perhaps, because he had the faculty of cutting through the elaborate nonessentials of a problem and of expressing the truth in words that the average man could understand. John Carter, of the *New York Times,* asserted that "perhaps Will Rogers has done more to educate the American public in world affairs than all the professors who have been elucidating the continental chaos since the Treaty of Versailles."[9] And S.S. Ratcliffe made the same observation: "After his first post-war tour of Europe, he delivered to American audiences, in the form of a two-hour lecture, as sound a lesson in international affairs as, I think, any public man was capable of giving at that time."[10]

Will's position in the line of crackerbox philosophers is difficult to evaluate, for he fits no convenient category. He was not a rural New England Yankee comedian like Jack Downing and Sam Slick; he had no political ax to grind like James Russell Lowell; he had no talent for political vituperation like Petroleum V. Nasby; he did not often play the fool character like Artemus Ward and Bill Nye; he wrote no sustained literature like Mark Twain; and he had no zeal for political and social reform like Martin Dooley. Yet, when he died, people of all stations in life spoke of his accidental death as though each had lost a dearly loved personal friend. This outburst of national sorrow was a tribute to the unique personality of the cowboy humorist who, despite wealth and fame, never lost the common touch; and his countrymen somehow seemed to have known it.

Will was the last of the crackerbox philosophers in the old tradition; and, with his death, the horse-sense tradition of American humor virtually ended. This homespun type of humor played out because of the changing pattern of American life in recent years. With the rise of mass education and the urbanization of society, sophisticated comedy has tended to replace rural humor. Moreover, the American public may no longer feel the need for the purgatives of the common-sense humorist, but it can still enjoy the common-sense pronouncements of Will Rogers which are often applicable to current problems that concern the American people.

Notes and References

Chapter One

1. Betty Rogers, *Will Rogers* (New York, 1942), pp. 34-38. Also Donald Day, *Will Rogers* (New York, 1962), pp. 5-7. Biographical material was taken from these books which are considered to be the most complete and accurate sources on Will's life.
2. *Autobiography of Will Rogers* (Boston, 1949), p. 21.
3. *Day,* Will Rogers, p. 46.
4. *Ibid.,* p. 57.
5. *Ibid.*
6. Will Rogers, Jr., Interview in Claremore, Oklahoma, April 12, 1957.
7. John Crawford, "Will Rogers," *New York Times,* December 14, 1924.
8. *The Illiterate Digest* (New York, 1924), pp. 164-65.
9. *The Cowboy Philosopher on the Peace Conference* (New York, 1919), p. 56.
10. Day, *Will Rogers,* pp. 129-30.
11. Betty Rogers, *Will Rogers,* p. 194.
12. Will Rogers, Jr., Interview in Claremore, Oklahoma; James Rogers, Interview in Tulsa, Oklahoma.
13. *Ibid.*
14. Betty Rogers, *Will Rogers,* pp. 309-10.

Chapter Two

1. Homer Croy, *Our Will Rogers* (New York, Little Brown), p. 107.
2. Day, *Will Rogers,* p. 68.
3. *Ibid.,* p. 84.
4. *Ibid.,* p. 79.
5. Anon., *New York Times,* July 1, 1917, p. 6.
6. *Cowboy Philosopher on the Peace Conference,* p. 31.
7. *Ibid.,* p. 33.
8. *Ibid.,* p. 41.

9. *Ibid.*, p. 47.

10. *Ibid.*, p. 41.

11. *Ibid.*, pp. 56-57.

12. *Cowboy Philosopher on Prohibition* (New York, 1919), p. 32.

13. *Ibid.*, p. 32.

14. "The Gossip Shop," *Bookman* L (November-December, 1919), 3-4.

15. *Autobiography of Will Rogers*, pp. 70-71.

16. Day, *Will Rogers*, pp. 127-28.

17. Betty Rogers, *Will Rogers*, p. 154.

Chapter Three

1. Day, *Autobiography of Will Rogers*, pp. xv-xvi.

2. L.H. Robbins, "Portrait of An American Philosopher," *New York Times*, November 3, 1935.

3. Day, *Will Rogers*, p. 97.

4. *Ibid.*, p. 112.

5. David McCord, "Review of *Illiterate Digest*," *Saturday Review of Literature* (February 21, 1925), 540.

6. *Sanity is Where You Find It* (New York, 1955), pp. 4-5.

7. *Ibid.*, p. 37.

8. *Ibid.*, p. 107.

9. *Ibid.*, p. 141.

10. *Ibid.*, p. 237.

11. *Autobiography of Will Rogers*, p. 238.

12. "Book Review," *Nation*, CXX (February 11, 1925), 160.

13. *Autobiography of Will Rogers*, p. 336.

14. *Ibid.*, p. 302

15. *Ibid.*, p. 336.

16. *Ibid.*, p. 111.

17. *Ibid.*, pp. 320-21.

18. J. T. Winterich, "Simon Pure Rogersana," *Saturday Review of Literature* XXXII (October 15, 1949), 19.

19. *Sanity Is Where You Find It*, p. 99.

20. *Autobiography of Will Rogers*, p. 180.

21. *Ibid.*, pp. 199-200.

22. *Ibid.*, p. 209.

23. *Ibid.*, p. 212.

24. *Ibid.*, p. 214.

25. *Ibid.*, p. 228.

26. *Ibid.*, p. 299.

27. *Ibid.*, pp. 238-39.

28. *Sanity Is Where You Find It*, p. 150.

29. *Autobiography of Will Rogers*, p. 315.

30. *Sanity Is Where You Find It*, p. 181.

31. Day, *Autobiography of Will Rogers*, p. 324.
32. *Ibid.*, p. 325.
33. *Ibid.*, p. 393.
34. *Ibid.*, p. 387.
35. *Ibid.*, p. 81.
36. *Ibid.*, pp. 86-88.
37. *Ibid.*
38. Paula Love, *The Will Rogers Book* (New York, 1961), p. 183.
39. *Ibid.*, pp. 184-85.
40. *Sanity Is Where You Find It*, pp. 48-49.
41. *Ibid.*
42. *Ibid.*
43. *Ibid.*, pp. 50-51.
44. *How We Elect Our Presidents* (Boston, 1940), p. 19.
45. *Ibid.*, p. 33.
46. *Ibid.*, pp. 38-39.
47. *Ibid.*, pp. 39-40.
48. *Ibid.*, p. 44.
49. *Ibid.*, pp. 66-67.
50. *Ibid.*, p. 69.
51. *Ibid.*, pp. 74-75.
52. *Ibid.*, p. 78.
53. *Ibid.*, p. 88.
54. *Ibid.*
55. *Ibid.*, p. 117.
56. *Ibid.*, p. 119.
57. *Ibid.*, pp. 122-23.
58. Norris Yates, *The American Humorists* (Iowa State Press, 1964), p. 120.

Chapter Four
1. Love, *The Will Rogers Book*, p. 63.
2. *Autobiography of Will Rogers*, pp. 103-04.
3. *Ibid.*, pp. 116-17.
4. *Sanity Is Where You Find It*, p. 46.
5. *Ibid.*, p. 47.
6. *Ibid.*
7. *Ibid.*
8. *Ibid.*, p. 52.
9. *Ibid.*, p. 97.
10. *Letters of a Self-Made Diplomat to His President* (New York, 1926), pp. 239-40.
11. *Ibid.*, pp. 244-45.
12. *Autobiography of Will Rogers*, p. 222.

13. *Sanity Is Where You Find It*, p. 121.
14. *Autobiography of Will Rogers*, p. 222.
15. *Ibid.*, p. 264.
16. *Ibid.*, p. 274.
17. *Sanity Is Where You Find It*, pp. 153-54.
18. *Autobiography of Will Rogers*, pp. 271-72.
19. *Ibid.*, p. 280.
20. *Sanity Is Where You Find It*, p. 161.
21. *Autobiography of Will Rogers*, p. 304.
22. *Ibid.*, pp. 144-45.
23. *Ibid.*, p. 255.
24. *Ibid.*, p. 319.
25. *Sanity Is Where You Find It*, pp. 230-31.
26. *Autobiography of Will Rogers*, p. 378.
27. *Ibid.*, p. 389.
28. Letter to Clem Rogers dated April 13, 1902. Original destroyed when the home of Mr. Sallie McSpadden burned in 1932. Duplicated copy in Will Rogers Museum.
29. *Letters of a Self-Made Diplomat to His President*, p. 71.
30. *Ibid.*, p. 64.
31. *Ibid.*, p. 82.
32. *Ibid.*, pp. 48-49.
33. *Ibid.*, pp. 101-11.
34. *Ibid.*, p. 114.
35. *The Will Rogers Book*, p. 64.
36. *Letters of a Self-Made Diplomat to His President*, p. 143.
37. *Ibid.*, pp. 146-47.
38. *Ibid.*
39. *Ibid.*, p. 178.
40. *Ibid.*, p. 167.
41. *Ibid.*, p. 157.
42. *Ibid.*, pp. 160-61.
43. *Ibid.*, p. 171.
44. *Ibid.*
45. *Ibid.*, p. 175.
46. *Ibid.*, p. 120.
47. *Ibid.*, p. 118.
48. *Ibid.*, p. 180.
49. *There's Not a Bathing Suit in Russia* (New York, 1927), p. 93.
50. *Ibid.*, pp. 94-95.
51. *Ibid.*, p. 88.
52. *Autobiography of Will Rogers*, p. 160.
53. *There's Not a Bathing Suit in Russia*, pp. 140-42.
54. *Ibid.*, p. 97.

55. *Ibid.*, p. 99.
56. *Ibid.*, p. 100.
57. *Ibid.*, pp. 146-47.
58. *Ibid.*, p. 136.
59. *Ibid.*, p. 72.
60. *Ibid.*, p. 150.
61. *Sanity Is Where You Find It*, p. 215.
62. *Ibid.*, p. 216.
63. *Ibid.*, pp. 217-18.
64. *Ibid.*, p. 46.
65. *Autobiography of Will Rogers*, pp. 165-66.
66. Day, *Will Rogers.*
67. *Autobiography of Will Rogers*, p. 170.
68. *Ibid.*, p. 170.
69. *Ibid.*, p. 172.
70. *Sanity Is Where You Find It*, p. 86.
71. *Autobiography of Will Rogers*, p. 268.
72. *Ibid.*, pp. 268-69.
73. *New York Times*, Feb. 11, 1933.
74. Gilbert Seldes, "The Death of Satire," *New Republic* XLIX *(Jan. 5, 1927), 16.*

Chapter Five
1. *Autobiography of Will Rogers*, pp. 303-04.
2. *Ibid.*
3. "The Cowboy Philosopher," *New Republic* LXXXIII *(August 25, 1955), 62.*
4. Betty Rogers, *Will Rogers.*
5. Croy, *Our Will Rogers*, p. 185.
6. *Autobiography of Will Rogers*, p. 229.
7. *Ibid.*, p. 222.
8. *Ibid.*, p. 144.
9. *Sanity Is Where You Find It*, pp. 150-51.
10. *Ibid.*, p. 17.
11. *Ibid.*, p. 56.
12. *Illiterate Digest*, p. 229.
13. *Autobiography of Will Rogers*, p. 241.
14. *Ibid.*, p. 325.
15. *Ibid.*, p. 98.
16. *Ibid.*, p. 100.
17. *Sanity Is Where You Find It*, p. 93.
18. Max Eastman, *Enjoyment of Laughter* (New York, 1948), pp. 123-24.
19. George Martin, "The Wit of Will Rogers," *American* LXXXVIII *(November, 1919), 34.*

20. Eastman, *Enjoyment of Laughter,* p. 213.
21. Martin, "The Wit of Will Rogers," p. 106.
22. *Ibid.,* p. 34.

Chapter Six

1. Henry S. Canby, "Homespun Philosopher," *Saturday Review of Literature* XII (August 30, 1935), 8.
2. Walter Blair, *Horse Sense in American Humor* (Chicago, 1942), pp. vi-vii.
3. *Ibid.,* p. 196.
4. *Ibid.,* pp. 197-202.
5. Fredrick Van de Water, "Books and So Forth," *New York Herald Tribune* (January 5, 1925).
6. Elmer Ellis, *Mr. Dooley's America* (New York, 1941), p. 106.
7. *Horse Sense in American Humor,* p. 273.
8. S.S. Ratcliffe, "Will Rogers," CLV *Spectator* (August 23, 1935), 288.
9. John Carter, "Book Review," *New York Times* (October 31, 1926).
10. Ratcliffe, "Will Rogers," 288.

Selected Bibliography

PRIMARY SOURCES

1. Books

Rogers, Will. *The Cowboy Philosopher on the Peace Conference.* New York: Harper and Bros., 1919.
————. *The Cowboy Philosopher on Prohibition.* New York: Harper and Bros., 1919.
————. *The Illiterate Digest.* New York: Albert and Charles Boni, 1919.
————. *Letters of a Self-Made Diplomat to His President.* New York: Albert and Charles Boni, 1926.
————. *There's Not a Bathing Suit in Russia.* New York: Albert and Charles Boni, 1927.
————. *Ether and Me.* New York: G.P. Putnam, 1929.
————. *Wit and Philosophy from the Radio Talks of America's Humorist.* Chicago, 1930.
————. *Autobiography of Will Rogers.* Edited by Donald Day. Boston: Houghton Mifflin, 1949.
————. *How We Elect Our Presidents.* Edited by Donald Day. New York: Little, Brown, 1952.
————. *Sanity Is Where You Find It.* Edited by Donald Day. New York: Houghton Mifflin, 1955.
————. *The Will Rogers Book.* Edited by Paula McSpadden Love. Indianapolis: Bobbs-Merrill, 1961.

2. Columns

Sunday column for the McNaught Syndicate from December 31, 1922 to August 11, 1935. Carried by the *New York Times.*
Daily column for the McNaught Syndicate from October 15, 1926 to August 15, 1935. Carried by the *New York Times.*

3. Periodicals

————. "Bacon, Beans and Limousines," *Survey,* LXVII (November 15, 1931), 185.

————. "Bucking a Headwind," *Saturday Evening Post,* CC (January 28, 1928), 6-7.

————. "Coolidge," *American,* LVII (January, 1929), 20-21.

————. "Corn Whiskey, Courage and Commerce," *American,* CIX (May, 1930), 69.

————. "Duck Al — Here's a Letter," *Saturday Evening Post,* CC (October 29, 1927), 3-4.

————. "Florida Versus California," *Saturday Evening Post,* CXCVIII (May 29, 1926), 10-11.

————. "Flying and Eating My Way from Coast to Coast," *Saturday Evening Post,* CC (January 21, 1938), 3-4.

————. "Grand Champion," *American,* CVIII (December, 1929), 34.

————. "Hole in One," *Saturday Evening Post,* CC (November 5, 1927), 6.

————. "Hoofin' Kid from Claremore," *American,* CVII (April, 1927), 34.

————. "How to be Funny," *American,* CVIII (September, 1929), 61.

————. "Letter to the Philippines," *Saturday Evening Post,* CCIV (April 30, 1932), 6-7.

————. "Mr. Toastmaster and Democrats," *Saturday Evening Post,* CCI (March 30, 1929), 3-5.

————. "My Rope and Gun for a Democratic Issue," *Saturday Evening Post,* CCI (March 30, 1929), 3-5.

————. "My Rope and Gun for a Democratic Issue," *Saturday Evening Post,* CXCVIII (May 1, 1926), 3-4.

————. "On China," *China,* XL (April 23, 1927), 201.

————. "On the Situation," *China,* LIX (January 2, 1932), 143.

————. "There's Life in the Old Gal Yet," *Saturday Evening Post,* CCI (January 19, 1929), 6-7.

SECONDARY SOURCES

1. Books

ALLEN. FREDRICK LEWIS. *Only Yesterday.* New York: Bantam Giant Edition, 1952. Social history of the United States during the decade 1920-30.

BLAIR, WALTER. *Horse Sense In American Humor.* Chicago: University of Chicago Press, 1952. Perceptive study of American humor which places Will Rogers as crackerbox philosopher in the tradition of Downing, Ward, Dooley, *et al.*

————. *Native American Humor: 1800-1900.* San Francisco: Chandler Press: 1960. Brief history of American humor including excerpts of leading nineteenth-century humorists.

COBB, IRVIN S. *Exit Laughing.* New York: Bobbs-Merrill, 1941. Personal recollections of Will Rogers by one of his close friends, himself a popular humorist.

CROY, HOMER. *Our Will Rogers.* New York: Duell, Sloan and Pearce, 1953. Readable account of Will's life. Highly informative about career in Hollywood as movie star.

DALE, EDWARD, and WARDELL, MORRIS. *History of Oklahoma.* New York, 1948. Standard history of the State of Oklahoma; includes account of the Cherokee Nation prior to statehood.

DAY, DONALD. *Will Rogers.* New York: David McKay Co., Inc., 1962. Most thorough, accurate biography that has been published.

EASTMAN, MAX. *Enjoyment of Laughter.* New York: Simon and Schuster, 1948. Useful general analysis of humor; specifically comments on "timeliness" as the central ingredient of Rogers' humor.

ELLIS, ELMER. *Mr. Dooley's America.* New York: Alfred A. Knopf, Inc., 1941. Critical biography of Finley Peter Dunne (Mr. Dooley) whose humorous career overlapped that of Will Rogers.

HARMON, S.W. *Hell on the Border.* Fort Smith, Arkansas, 1902. Early classic of the American West; describes lawlessness of Oklahoma territory from 1878-1907.

HITCH, A.M. *Cadet Days of Will Rogers.* Boonville: Kemper Military School Publication, 1935. Informative pamphlet concerning Will's brief stay at Kemper Military School; describes his activities; gives comments of his former classmates.

LEACOCK, STEPHEN. *The Great Pages of American Humor.* New York, 1936. Collection of American humor; informative preface by a prominent Canadian humorist.

MILAM, IRENE MCSPADDEN. *Will Rogers as I Knew Him.* Claremore, Oklahoma, 1935. Recollections of Will by one of his sisters; interesting comments on his early life.

MILSTEN, DAVID. *An Appreciation of Will Rogers.* San Antonio: Naylor Company, 1935. General account of Will's life; praises him as a humanitarian as well as a humorist.

O'BRIEN, PATRICK J. *Will Rogers.* Philadelphia: John C. Winston, 1935. Popular presentation of Will Rogers; emphasizes his role as "spokesman" of the American people.

PAYNE, WILLIAM H., and LYONS, JAKE, editors. *Folks Say of Will Rogers.* New York: Putnam, 1936. Collection of eulogies and recollections of Rogers by diverse writers.

ROGERS, BETTY (MRS. WILL). *Will Rogers.* New York: Bobbs-Merrill Co., 1941. Mrs. Will Rogers' story of her husband's life; highly informative on Will's life and early career.

ROURKE, CONSTANCE. *American Humor.* New York: Harcourt, Brace & World, Inc., 1931. Classic discussion of the origin and nature of American humor.

TANDY, JENNETTE. *Crackerbox Philosophers in American Humor and Satire.* New York: Columbia University Press, 1925. Study of the persistence of the unlettered philosophers in American humor and the way in which they shaped American thought.

TRENT, SPI M. *My Cousin, Will Rogers.* New York: G.P. Putnam's Sons, 1939. Recollections of Will's early life by his cousin.

YATES, NORRIS. *The American Humorist.* Ames, Iowa: Iowa State University Press, 1964. Study of American humor in which Will's role as an "opinion maker" is challenged.

2. Periodicals

ANNONYMOUS. "Book Review," *Nation,* CXX (February 11, 1925), 160. A review of the *Illiterate Digest;* commentary on variety of his humorous techniques.

———. "Clown Becomes a Nuisance," *American,* CXIV (October 22, 1932), 55. Attack upon Will Rogers for his remarks during the 1932 political conventions and campaigns.

———. "The Cowboy Philosopher," *New Republic,* LXXXIII (August 28, 1935), 62. Obituary reporting universality of the impact of Will's death.

———. "The Gossip Shop," *Bookman,* L (November-December, 1919), 3-4. Review of Will Rogers' first book *Cowboy Philosopher on the Peace Conference.*

———. "King Will," *Commonweal,* XVII (December 14, 1932), 173. Comments on Will Rogers' prestige as a columnist and warning him to report accurately and completely on political affairs.

BLAIR, WALTER. "Burlesque in Nineteenth Century Humor," *American Literature,* (November, 1930), 236-47. Scholarly analysis of the nineteenth-century humorist who employed burlesque as a technique.

BLANCHARD, EDWIN. "Book Review," New York *Sun* (May 28, 1927). Review of *Letters of a Self Made Diplomat to His President,* comments on Will's analysis of European politics.

BOYNTON, H.W. "American Humor," *Atlantic Monthly,* XC (September, 1902). Suggests that American humorists are like the court jesters whose remarks are tolerated because of the manner in which their ideas are presented.

BUTTERFIELD, ROGER. "Legend of Will Rogers," *Life,* XXVII (July 18, 1949), 78-81. Popular account of Will Rogers as the humorist is remembered through his movies and his oft repeated aphorisms which have become part of American folklore.

CANBY, HENRY. S. "Homespun Philosophers," *Saturday Review of Literature,* XII (August 31, 1935), 8. Review of the crackerbox philosophers in American literary history; refers to Rogers as the last genuine humorist in the tradition.

CARTER, JOHN. "Book Review," *New York Times,* Book Review Section (October 31, 1926), 8. Review of *Letters of a Self-made Diplomat to His President;* comments favorably on Will's political analysis of conditions in Europe.

CRAWFORD, JOHN. "Will Rogers," *New York Times* (December 14, 1925). Review of Will Rogers as a humorist in the Ziegfeld Follies.

LARDNER, RING. "With a Gun and Rope," *Colliers,* LXXXIII (February 2, 1929). Commentary on Rogers as a political candidate.

MARTIN, GEORGE. "The Wit of Will Rogers," *American,* LXXXVII (November, 1919), 34. Analysis of Will's humor; calls attention to timeliness and brevity as the chief ingredients of his wit.

RATCLIFFE, S.S. "Will Rogers," *Spectator,* CLV (August 23, 1935), 287-8. British view of Will Rogers; comments on the unique political sense of Will Rogers during his lecture series in England.

ROBBINS, L.H. "Portrait of an American Philosopher," *New York Times* (November 3, 1935). Describes Will Rogers' political philosophy as characteristic of Middle American, sometimes shrewd, sometimes naive.

SELDES, GILBERT. "The Death of Satire," *New Republic,* XLIX (January 5, 1927), 193. Includes a discussion of Will Rogers as a political satirist whose effect is blunted by the variety of media which he uses and the size of the audience to whom his humor is directed.

VAN de WATER, FREDRICK. "Book and So Forth," *New York Herald Tribune* (January 5, 1925). Compares Mark Twain and Will Rogers. Twain infinitely superior except in short paragraphs where Rogers often equals the elder humorist.

WINTERICH, J.T. "Simon Pure Rogersana," *Saturday Review of Literature,* (October 15, 1949), 19. Review of *Autobiography of Will Rogers,* edited by Donald Day.

Index